Robert C. Andringa
with Outi Flynn and Sandra R. Sabo

Nonprofit Board

ANSWER BOOK II

Beyond the Basics

BOARDSOURCE
Building Effective Nonprofit Boards

Formerly the National Center for Nonprofit Boards

Library of Congress Cataloging-in-Publication Data

Andringa, Robert C.
    Nonprofit Board Answer Book II: Beyond the Basics
    by Robert C. Andringa, with Outi Flynn and Sandra R. Sabo.
    p. cm.
Includes bibliographical references and index.
    ISBN 1-58686-063-1
1.Nonprofit organizations—Management. 2. Directors of
corporations. I. Flynn, Outi. II. Sabo, Sandra. III. Title
    HD62.6 .A5 2002
    658.4'22—dc21
  2002008688

BOARDSOURCE
Building Effective Nonprofit Boards

BoardSource, formerly the National Center for Nonprofit Boards, is the premier resource for practical information, tools and best practices, training, and leadership development for board members of nonprofit organizations worldwide. Through our highly acclaimed programs and services, BoardSource enables organizations to fulfill their missions by helping build strong and effective nonprofit boards.

BoardSource provides assistance and resources to nonprofit leaders through workshops, publishing, training, and our extensive Web site, www.boardsource.org. A team of BoardSource governance consultants works directly with nonprofit leaders to design specialized solutions to meet an organization's needs. BoardSource is the world's largest, most comprehensive publisher of materials on nonprofit governance, offering more than 100 booklets, books, videos, CDs, and audiotapes. BoardSource assists nongovernmental organizations throughout the world through partnerships and capacity building. Each year, BoardSource hosts the National Leadership Forum, bringing together approximately 800 board members and chief executives of nonprofit organizations from around the world.

Created out of the nonprofit sector's critical need for governance guidance and expertise, BoardSource is a 501(c)(3) nonprofit organization that has provided practical solutions to nonprofit organizations of all sizes in diverse communities. In 2001, BoardSource changed its name from the National Center for Nonprofit Boards to better reflect its mission. Today, BoardSource has more than 15,000 members and has served more than 75,000 nonprofit leaders.

For more information, please visit our Web site www.boardsource.org, e-mail us at mail@boardsource.org, or call us at 800-883-6262.

HAVE YOU USED THESE BOARDSOURCE RESOURCES?

VIDEOS

Meeting the Challenge: An Orientation to Nonprofit Board Service

Blueprint for Success: A Guide to Strategic Planning for Nonprofit Board Members

Speaking of Money: A Guide to Fund-Raising for Nonprofit Board Members

Building a Successful Team: A Guide to Nonprofit Board Development

BOOKS

The Board Chair Handbook

Managing Conflicts of Interest: Practical Guidelines for Nonprofit Boards

Checks and Balances: The Board Member's Guide to Nonprofit Financial Audits

The Board-Savvy CEO: How To Build a Strong, Positive Relationship with Your Board

Presenting: Board Orientation

Presenting: Nonprofit Financials

The Board Meeting Rescue Kit: 20 Ideas for Jumpstarting Your Board Meetings

The Board Building Cycle: Nine Steps to Finding, Recruiting, and Engaging Nonprofit Board Members

The Policy Sampler: A Resource for Nonprofit Boards

To Go Forward, Retreat! The Board Retreat Handbook

Nonprofit Board Answer Book: Practical Guide for Board Members and Chief Executives

The Legal Obligations of Nonprofit Boards

Self-Assessment for Nonprofit Governing Boards

Assessment of the Chief Executive

Fearless Fund-Raising

The Nonprofit Board's Guide to Bylaws

Creating and Using Investment Policies

Transforming Board Structure: New Possibilities for Committees and Task Forces

THE GOVERNANCE SERIES

1. *Ten Basic Responsibilities of Nonprofit Boards (available on audiotape)*
2. *The Chief Executive's Role in Developing the Nonprofit Board*
3. *Creating Strong Board–Staff Partnerships*
4. *The Chair's Role in Leading the Nonprofit Board*
5. *How To Help Your Board Govern More and Manage Less (available on audiotape)*
6. *The Board's Role in Strategic Planning (available on audiotape)*
7. *Financial Responsibilities of the Nonprofit Board*
8. *Understanding Nonprofit Financial Statements*
9. *Fund-Raising and the Nonprofit Board Member (available on audiotape)*
10. *Evaluation and the Nonprofit Board*

For an up-to-date list of publications and information about current prices, membership, and other services, please call BoardSource at 800-883-6262.

Contents

Part III: Strategic Alliances

Part IV: In the Public Eye

Part V: Board–Staff Partnerships

Preface

The earlier *Nonprofit Board Answer Book* was written primarily for board members. In that book, Ted Engstrom and I discussed the distinct roles of board and staff. We tried to focus on the governance functions of board members, the structure of boards and committees, and other principles of good governance.

This book looks at nonprofit organizations from a different perspective. Here I focus on some of the broader challenges, issues, and trends in the nonprofit world that should capture the attention of both board and staff. In some organizations, board members — wearing either their governance hats or their volunteer hats — often drive how the board deals with the challenges presented in this book. In other organizations, staff bring these issues to the board.

This *Nonprofit Board Answer Book II: Beyond the Basics* book differs from its companion in at least three ways. First, I wrote this book for both board members and senior staff, especially the staff who develop board proposals or have responsibilities for implementing board policies. Second, this book addresses major challenges and issues that are typically worked out with a great deal of interaction between both board and staff, with the leadership coming from each group. Third, this book includes dozens of specific examples from nonprofit organizations that sometimes reflect good practices and sometimes remind us of how wrong things can go without proper board leadership.

I am deeply indebted to Sandra Sabo, whose research and writing skills brought together a mass of conceptual and technical information to give breadth and depth to the 17 chapters. Her understanding of nonprofit organizations and writing skills are outstanding. We hope our work will take your board to new levels of accomplishment, with the result that both the board and the staff feel empowered to do their respective jobs with more confidence and effectiveness.

The nonprofit sector is getting more competitive while the world around us changes faster each year. This is no time to relax nor to feel that non-profit organizations have discovered all there is to know about effective-ness. Because, in the end, our mission is to change lives for the better, we must stay up to date on strategies that might take us to the next level of significance. My hope is that *Answer Book II* will be a timely catalyst for moving your organization forward.

Both Sandy and I are indebted to the professional staff at BoardSource who encouraged us in doing this book and in providing much of the information that we hope will now take you beyond your current dreams for your organization.

Robert C. Andringa

August 2002

Foreword

"Where was the board?" "How could the board have allowed this to happen?" "Why didn't the board know?" Such questions have become all too frequent as a growing number of nonprofit (and for-profit) organizations find themselves mired in financial and ethical trouble that, in hindsight, could have been avoided.

In the past, the public and media typically held the nonprofit organization's chief executive solely responsible for any problems that arose. Increasingly, the public and media have begun to recognize that in addition to the chief executive, the nonprofit organization's board is legally and ethically charged with maintaining effective board governance and oversight for every facet of the nonprofit organization's operations. Today, being asked to serve on a nonprofit board is more than a ceremonial honor or a fundraising obligation but rather a responsibility to see to it that the nonprofit organization fulfills its legal and moral obligations to employees, clients, donors, and the general public.

Unfortunately, while there is increasing recognition of the critical role of board governance and oversight, there is no general agreement or understanding about how to educate and train board members to fulfill these board responsibilities. This should not be surprising. Trustees are often selected based on their connections to current or former trustees or their potential to raise funds on behalf of the nonprofit organization. While these are valid criteria for considering potential trustees, they do not give any indication of the individual's board I.Q. — his or her knowledge and understanding of appropriate nonprofit board governance.

Achieving effective board governance is further complicated because nonprofit organizations at different stages of development require board members who bring different skills and abilities. Smaller nonprofit organizations with limited budgets rely on board trustees to function as staff. In larger nonprofit organizations with full-time staff, board trustees must often have specialized skills to provide effective oversight. The standard for what constitutes effective nonprofit board governance (and the requisite skills required of trustees) is different depending on the budget, staffing, and purpose of the nonprofit organization. All of these factors contribute to the difficulty of providing the appropriate level of board training and education to trustees.

Answer Book II by Robert C. Andringa with Outi Flynn and Sandra R. Sabo is an important contribution to the development of best practices for nonprofit governance. The book examines a wide range of topics that are essential for effective governance that should be of great interest to nonprofit trustees and staff. Specifically, the book examines several of the toughest challenges faced by nonprofit organizations as they relate to organizational mission and purpose, finances, strategic alliances, public relations, and board-staff relationships.

Of particular interest are the chapters on balancing mission and accountability and the relationship between the chief executive and board chair. The book's analysis of the board's ongoing responsibility to continually balance the nonprofit organization's mission, organizational structure, and financial health is a valuable conceptual framework for understanding the responsibilities of the board. The framework is also useful for showing how ignoring any one of these dimensions can result in significant trouble for a nonprofit organization. For example, an exclusive focus on financial health to the exclusion of organizational mission and structure creates an imbalance that, over time, erodes the stability of the nonprofit organization, placing it at risk for self-destruction.

The relationship between the board chair and chief executive is a key linchpin in the success or failure of nonprofit organizations. If the relationship is too cordial, there is the possibility that there will be inadequate board oversight. Conversely, if the relationship is too adversarial, the energy and momentum that should be directed to the success of the nonprofit organization is diverted as the board chair and chief executive spend more time at odds with each other rather than on achieving the organization's mission and goals. The book's advice that mutual trust, and agreeing to disagree, are important components of the board chair-chief executive relationship are critical messages that too many of those who occupy these positions either do not understand or have chosen to ignore.

Answer Book II is full of useful, easy-to-read information. As a result, readers are likely to use it as a desk reference and refer to it only when confronted with a difficult organizational challenge. This would be a mistake. The best use of this book is for nonprofit boards and staff to learn about and incorporate best practices for effective governance into their operations before problems arise and lead to irreparable harm to the organization. This is the next important step in the evolution of nonprofit board governance.

Emmet Carson

Emmett D. Carson, Ph.D., is president and chief executive of The Minneapolis Foundation.

Part I

Mission
and Purpose

1.
Balancing Mission and Accountability

As our organization has grown, a culture of accountability has developed, but sometimes it seems as though we focus more on the bureaucracy (how we do things) rather than on our mission (why and how effectively we do things). How can we strike a healthy balance?

Many nonprofit organizations get started when a small group of people rallies around a common cause or a charismatic, visionary leader who can articulate what needs to be done and why. Read the histories of most nonprofits and you'll find stories of conversations around kitchen tables, chance encounters, and phone calls across town or across the country, all of which galvanized a group into action. A sense of haphazardness, even controlled chaos, may characterize some groups in their early days, as people roll up their sleeves and do whatever needs to be done to fulfill and advance the mission.

In time, however, processes and procedures develop to ensure consistency as the ranks of volunteers expand. The organization becomes a legal entity, a board of directors is chosen, and programs and projects are formalized in a budget. Recognizing they can't do it all, board members hire one staff member who, in turn, hires others. Revenues start to grow, and activities expand accordingly.

As this development cycle continues and the organization grows in size and stature, the board naturally takes on more oversight responsibilities. It must also grapple with the tensions inherent in all nonprofit organizations: the pull of the mission (why we exist) versus the pull of structure (what we must have to succeed) versus the pull of financial support (what makes us attractive to funders). Go too far in any one direction, and you may pull the organization completely apart.

For example, the board of a New York based historical society announced its closing in 1993. Because leaders had perpetuated their predecessors' behavior over the years, concentrating on the present rather than the future, fiscal problems continually beset the society during its nearly 200 years in existence. Intent on preservation, the society did not make its collection readily available to the public or seek city support of its activities, which made fundraising nearly impossible. To generate much-needed funds the society sold works from its collection, which then raised ethical questions and a public outcry. The society had failed to consider how it could best benefit stakeholders.

DEFINING DUTIES

Without a doubt, the board is accountable for what the organization does. Board members must answer to the stakeholders the nonprofit serves, to funders, and to the public. To carry out their roles to the fullest extent, board members should address the issues described below.

UNDERSTAND BOARD AND STAFF ROLES

Distinguishing what is strategic (the board's role) and what is administrative (the staff's role) helps keep each party focused on its responsibilities. Board members who become involved in operations tend to lose objectivity about personnel, programs, and organizational performance. And chief executives who attempt to control policy development through withholding of critical information or sheer force of personality get in the way of board decision making.

Defining board (governance) and staff (management) boundaries sounds easier than it is. The responsibility for fund development, for example, may rest with a staff member, but board members are expected to play a significant role in that area. If an organization is experiencing internal turmoil or transition, the board may exert its leadership by implementing policy as well as developing it, but the board should accept such a hands-on role only as an interim measure.

Board oversight should not be confused with board interference. While boards are accountable for an organization's decisions, they are not responsible for managing the programs or the people who carry out those decisions. To clarify the distinction, the board and chief executive should openly discuss their roles and agree upon where to draw the line in each case. The discussion should be ongoing. Roles are sure to change as the organization evolves, grows, ages, and reinvents itself.

USE RESOURCES WISELY

The board has a responsibility to all stakeholders to ensure the organization operates efficiently by employing personnel and financial resources for maximum benefit.

AVOID BEING A RUBBER STAMP

Before casting your vote, read the background materials, analyze the statistics, listen carefully to presentations, and ask pointed questions about stakeholders' needs, relevance to mission, and success (or failure) of strategies. Put everything to the test, even if it is presented or recommended by a high-profile board member you admire, a long-serving staff member, or even the founder of the organization. Your opinion counts, too. Remember that you have legal, ethical, and moral responsibilities, all of which should overshadow any belief that you should keep silent if something troubles you. In fact, the board culture should welcome open debate and discussion with the caveat that any decision the board makes should be publicly supported by all of its members, even those who personally disagree.

DECISIONS, DECISIONS

In the course of a meeting, board members and the chief executive may have to grapple with several complex issues that have long-term implications for the organization. To ensure an appropriate amount of thought and analysis have been devoted to each decision, consider using a checklist like the one below.

- Have we accurately defined the issue or problem from the perspective of various stakeholders?

- Would we define the issue differently if we looked at it from an outsider's perspective?

- How did this situation occur?

- Is there anything in our organizational culture that made it easier for this situation to develop?

If you reach the point where you don't feel you have time to attend meetings or read board materials thoroughly, do the organization a favor and resign. Then the organization can appoint someone else better able to fulfill the myriad responsibilities of board service.

COMPLY WITH FEDERAL AND STATE LAWS

Because it requires public disclosure of nonprofit income and expenses, the Internal Revenue Service Form 990 is seen as the chief means of keeping boards accountable to both the government (which grants tax-exempt status) and the general public. In addition, each state has laws that require nonprofits to register or report their activities in certain areas. (See Chapter 12 for more information.)

PUBLISH AN ANNUAL REPORT

This document doesn't have to be fancy, but it should include your mission, specific programs and their accomplishments, names of leaders, and audited financial statements. Distribute it widely, opening up your organization for all to see. The more open you are about how your board does business, the more likely people are to feel that their trust in the organization is well-placed.

- What opportunities does this situation present?
- What is the intended result of the decision?
- Whom could this decision or action benefit? Injure?
- Are we confident the decision would be as valid in five or 10 years as it seems today?
- Would each of us, as individuals, have any qualms about disclosing or explaining the decision to a spouse, boss, family member, stakeholder in the organization, or society as a whole?
- What is the potential for the decision being misunderstood?
- What are the implications in terms of corporate image and board members' personal image?
- How can our organization identify and generate additional opportunities arising from this and other situations?

MANAGE THE RISKS

Board members may be held liable for actions they took — or should have made sure others took — on behalf of the organization. Risk management includes purchasing directors and officers insurance, overseeing the establishment of adequate internal controls, and understanding the legal and fiscal responsibilities of board service. (See Chapter 12 for more information.)

ADOPT A CONFLICT-OF-INTEREST POLICY

Board members who stand to benefit in some way from a policy or decision need to disclose that possibility. Even the hint of personal gain by leaders or their families can raise stakeholders' doubts about leaders' judgment and prompt public censure of your organization. (See Chapter 13 for more information.)

DEVELOP A CODE OF ETHICS

Both board and staff members should adhere to standards of conduct that reflect personal and organizational integrity. A code of ethics, for example, may encompass conflict-of-interest issues (disclosure of family and personal relationships), financial issues (compensation or reimbursement of board members), and fundraising practices, as well as spell out the consequences of violating the standards. Like all board policies, the code of ethics should be revisited periodically and updated to reflect changes in the internal and external environments.

ESTABLISH A GIFT POLICY

Although most contributions arrive in the form of checks, some donors prefer to make a gift of stock, real estate, or even artwork. If your organization does not have staff with an expertise in planned giving, such bequests may be more trouble than they appear to be worth, especially if the donor restricts their sale or use. Should an individual or foundation place restrictions on a gift that is accepted, the board has an obligation to respect the donor's wishes and see that the organization complies fully with the request.

Having a policy that states any contribution must be related to the organization's mission will keep you on course. It can be tempting to accept a large donation that takes your nonprofit in a new direction, but doing so may have serious consequences. If the new initiative doesn't square with the strategic plan, for instance, you may drain resources from bedrock programs just to satisfy the donor and confuse (or alienate) other donors in the process.

MONITOR EXECUTIVE COMPENSATION

Make sure your organization has a process in place to evaluate the chief executive and determine his or her salary and benefits. All board members must be aware of the chief executive's compensation package or risk being blindsided if allegations of outrageous benefits or inappropriate perquisites arise among stakeholders or the media.

NURTURE NEW LEADERS

Boards that become too insular, either by electing the same people to leadership positions or by selecting new members in their same mold, can easily miss opportunities to strengthen the organization by introducing fresh perspectives and diverse voices. Consider instituting term limits, especially for top leadership positions. That ensures you keep injecting new enthusiasm and ideas into the board and don't burn out devoted stakeholders.

Assist the governance (nominating) committee by providing names of people you believe would bring needed expertise or diversity (gender, age, ethnic, or geographic) to the board. Funders and the community at large will look at your board as a reflection of the entire organization. If they perceive you are stuck in a rut or out of touch with what's happening in the wider world, they are more likely to lend their support elsewhere.

ALL THINGS CONSIDERED

With all these responsibilities on their minds, board members may lose sight of why they are there in the first place: to fulfill the organization's mission. As a gentle reminder, one nonprofit prints its mission statement on the back of board members' tablecards so they have no choice but to look at it during meetings. Another group prints its mission at the top of every agenda and posts it on a wall plaque in the boardroom, again to keep it top-of-mind.

Yet even a well-communicated mission, detailed financial reports, and an in-depth understanding of their roles are not enough to fulfill board members' accountability requirements. They also have to be willing to evaluate the organization's and their own performance. Ways to do this include

- developing a board calendar that includes the chief executive's evaluation, a board self-assessment, and a review of mission, vision, and objectives

- scheduling a board retreat every year or two to reflect on the mission and overall board functioning and to engage in the strategic planning process

- approving performance objectives tied to each part of the strategic plan, including targeted results and timetable for achieving them

TAKING A FRESH LOOK

Why?

That's a good question to pose in regard to any program or product your nonprofit offers. Most of them probably got started because it was the right thing to do at the time. But times change. And some programs and services might have been launched simply because they were pet projects of volunteer leaders in years past.

Without the pressures of the marketplace, which prompt for-profits to continually evaluate their offerings, nonprofits tend to perpetuate programs from one year to the next. Only a financial crisis or perhaps a leadership transition prods most nonprofits into taking a good look at the value of everything they offer. Yet money could be saved — or an even better program developed — if program evaluation were integrated into the board's strategic planning cycle.

Board members must answer to stakeholders about how wisely a group's resources are being employed and deployed. Consider appointing an evaluation team, consisting of volunteers and a staff liaison, to look at each program, gather relevant data, and ask the following questions:

- How does this program relate to our mission?

- When was it started?

- reviewing financial results and other measurable outcomes of programs with an eye toward ending those that do not contribute to a healthy bottom line

Most important, board members must be willing to say no to a project, a program, an initiative, a donor, a staff member, or even another board member with the potential to pull the organization away from its core values and purpose. When all is said and done, the public holds the governing board accountable for getting the job done ethically, efficiently, and effectively.

- What were the program's initial goals? Have those goals changed over time?

- What is the annual budget?

- What is the cost per member, client, or customer served?

- Why should we continue to do this? What are the tangible and intangible benefits?

- How successful is the program at meeting its goals?

- Is there another way we might achieve the same goals?

- What value does this program have in relation to the others? Where on the list does it rank?

- If this program should be continued, how might it be improved or combined with another initiative? What are the financial and staffing implications of those changes?

- If this program should be discontinued, what are the implications? What exit strategy should we employ (for example, phase it out or cease immediately)?

Develop an evaluation form to make the process as consistent as possible. Also, recruit team members who are able to be objective despite the subjective nature of the task. All should be willing to cast a critical eye at every product or service without protecting a sacred cow.

Words To Live By

Case in Point: United Way of America

Alexandria, Virginia

In the early 1990s, allegations of unethical behavior by its chief executive rocked United Way of America and the nonprofit world in general. Even before its former chief executive began serving a prison term for using the nonprofit's money to finance a lavish lifestyle, among other things, United Way launched a full-scale review of its entire structure and operations. The group ended up reducing staff by 25 percent and the budget by 30 percent, cutting out programs and functions that were not seen as essential to its mission, and instituting internal reforms related to finance and staff compensation.

United Way of America also appointed a board committee to develop a code of ethics. Applicable to all involved in the organization, the code of ethics is signed annually by all board and staff, who also provide feedback that is incorporated into future revisions.

The group's code of ethics includes these components:

- Preamble: a brief statement of the organization's mission and values.

- Personal integrity: a pledge to represent the organization in a fair and truthful manner.

- Professional excellence: model behaviors to follow, including respect for others, fair evaluation, and positive regard.

- Accountability and responsibilities: a statement of the organization's responsibilities to its constituents and their responsibilities to the organization, with an emphasis on good stewardship.

- Equal opportunity: the organization's commitment to attracting and maintaining a diverse workforce.

- Conflict of interest: each person's commitment to always act in the best interests of the organization and to evaluate personal conduct in terms of how others (especially the public) may perceive it.

To emphasize its commitment to ethical behavior, United Way of America also requires its affiliated organizations to have their own codes of ethics.

Suggested Action Steps

1. Review your organization's orientation for new board members, ensuring that it includes a clear explanation of roles, responsibilities, and accountability.

2. Revise your organization's code of ethics — or develop one — to cover personal integrity, professional excellence, responsibilities to stakeholders, and disclosure of any potential conflicts of interest.

3. Develop methods by which board members can periodically evaluate their own individual performance as well as that of the entire board structure and process.

2.

Rethinking the Organization

Times have changed, and other organizations have successfully entered our market. Plus, we've identified several new areas where we could potentially have an effect. Might it be time to reinvent the organization?

Successful nonprofit organizations use their mission statements as touchstones for everything they do. They ask, "Do the strategic plan and its supporting objectives build upon the whole reason we exist? Does the budget accurately reflect what's really important to us? Do our policies and procedures advance our purposes?"

There may come a time, however, when your mission statement no longer resonates with the people or community you serve, with donors, with the world in general. That may be perfectly acceptable to the leaders of an organization intended to go out of business after achieving its goals. After all, why perpetuate a nonprofit organization named Fight the Interstate after the eight-lane highway has been built elsewhere and victory declared?

More often, a mission statement becomes outdated or downright obsolete and leaders fail to realize it. The hints are probably there. Perhaps contributions have fallen off, media coverage is rare, registrations (and revenues) for long-popular events have decreased, volunteers are harder to find, another group with more charisma has appeared on the scene. Something is not quite right, yet the usual fixes — stepping up public relations activities, tinkering with program content or delivery, revising the strategic plan — don't do the trick.

It might be time to reinvent the organization, or it might not. You may simply need to place a priority on building brand identity or making branding efforts consistent throughout the organization. You'll know only if you revisit your organization's purpose and reassess its future direction.

ON A MISSION

Why does your organization exist? Ask employees, board members, and other stakeholders that question, and you may be surprised at the variety of responses. Some people may not be able to clearly define the mission; others may be totally off the mark or talk about *what* is offered (products and services) rather than the *why* behind those offerings.

If confusion about your mission is widespread, you need to review why your organization was created in the first place. If those needs still exist, revising (or simply rephrasing) the mission can clarify the organization's bedrock values for all parties involved. Another possibility is to put more effort into clearly communicating your mission as it stands, assuming it remains a valid statement of your organization's identity.

A good mission statement articulates an organization's fundamental purpose. Ideally, it is succinct (fewer than 30 words), memorable, and clear-cut, thus providing an easy answer to the elevator question, so, what does your group do, anyway? It is *not* a statement of strategies or programs. Here are some examples that illustrate the difference:

- *YES:* We want to stimulate love of learning and reading in young people.

- *NO:* Our mission is to provide free books to local schools.

- *YES:* To strengthen our community by helping those who are in need gain self-sufficiency.

- *NO:* To operate neighborhood-based food banks and offer job training.

Note that a mission statement differs from a *vision statement*. As its name implies, a vision statement paints a picture of what the organization sees possible in the future, often working with others having a similar vision but perhaps a different mission. Typically longer than a mission statement, a good vision statement is both idealistic and realistic: It challenges people to accomplish something while making the accomplishment attainable.

As an example, here's an excerpt of the vision statement adopted by the Wilder Foundation in St. Paul, Minnesota: "The Wilder Foundation's vision is a vibrant St. Paul, where individuals, families, and communities can prosper, with opportunities for all to be employed, to be engaged citizens, to live in decent housing, to attend good schools, and to receive support during times of need."

It's not uncommon for nonprofit organizations to revise their vision statements every three to five years, to reflect changes and developments in the world around them. And while mission statements change less frequently, they still need to be reviewed periodically, perhaps in conjunction with an organizational assessment or strategic planning session. Even if you don't change the mission statement, by keeping it top-of-mind you'll ensure that specific goals and objectives, as outlined in the strategic plan, flow directly from it.

SCANNING THE HORIZON

Let's assume your board of directors has helped develop and put its stamp of approval on a mission statement and perhaps a vision statement, too. With those as the guiding lights, you can more clearly see how your organization may need to change what it is or what it does in order to fulfill its primary purpose and realize its dreams.

If your organization typically waits for external change to occur, then reacts to it, you'll forever be playing catch-up. Conversely, staying on top of trends as they emerge and develop better positions your organization to keep pace with change. Below are the general areas to watch.

DEMOGRAPHICS

Every 10 years, the U.S. Census unveils the numbers that have a profound effect on how the country is governed (redistricting) and how federal funds are allocated, not to mention how the face of your typical stakeholder may be changing. For example, does your nonprofit concentrate on providing services to teenage boys? Demographic data will indicate whether the number of boys in that category will be higher or lower in the next five to ten years, where they are most likely to live, and what language they will primarily speak.

No Identity Crisis

Gut instinct may prompt board members to suggest a new name for your organization. Or perhaps the recommendation comes from staff or grass-roots volunteers who, having taken the pulse of the community, believe a new identity would reduce confusion or better communicate what you have to offer.

For example, one local nonprofit had for years operated a residence for homeless women and their children under the name Mary's Shelter. As low-cost housing grew scarce in the community, the women needed to stay for longer periods yet balked at doing so. When applying for employment or job training, they were reluctant to tell anyone they lived in a shelter; the term was politically loaded with negative connotations. The governing board took the hint and selected a new name for the residence that sounds like an upscale apartment building.

If you have decided to rebrand your organization with a new name (and perhaps communicate a new mission as well), here are some recommendations:

- **Test your theories.** Conduct focus groups with stakeholders to gauge their reactions to potential new names. You might work with a consulting firm that specializes in brand identification or do it yourself; one group even sent its staff out to ask people on the street to describe their reactions to a proposed name. As you winnow the list of possibilities, be sure to look at acronyms. People inevitably shorten a name, and you don't want your organization to be known by a nickname or a set of initials that isn't flattering.

- **Do your legal homework.** Contact your attorney to determine how the name change will affect the bylaws and official documents filed with the state and the Internal Revenue Service. Also seek the assistance of legal counsel to ensure your new name — including the Internet domain name you desire — is not trademarked or copyrighted by someone else.

- **Have a marketing plan.** Figure out how you will communicate the new name to your various constituencies, from donors to former board members to the media. In your plan, include strategies for reinforcing the new identity through broadcast e-mails, direct mail, newsletters, events, presentations, your Web site, and so forth.

As you craft the messages, be sensitive to the fact that long-time supporters may have an emotional attachment to the old name and feel somewhat betrayed by its disappearance. Explain the rationale behind the change, what the organization will gain, and what will stay the same.

- **Don't rush the rollout.** Schedule a minimum of 12 months (and a maximum of 18 months) for developing a new logo, phasing in its use, and redesigning everything from your Web site to the sign on your front door. You might need to come up with new, more relevant names for newsletters or special events. Lower-cost items such as stationery and business cards can change immediately, while publications and other materials can be reprinted when supplies dwindle. Invest in some stickers (maybe carrying the formerly known as . . . phrase) to update items in your inventory until they can be reprinted.

- **Pick a day.** Decide when the new name will take effect. You might time it to coincide with the start of the fiscal or calendar year, a significant anniversary, or a special event. When that day comes, retire the old identity gracefully yet swiftly.

ATTITUDES, PERCEPTIONS, AND BEHAVIORS

Census data also uncover generational shifts, such as baby boomers (born 1946 to 1964) starting to approach retirement age as the Millennials (born after 1981) enter the marketplace in full force. Each generation tends to have different characteristics in terms of work ethic, perspective on leisure, family values, and so forth. They are also shaped by large-scale economic or societal events, such as wars, recessions, and economic booms. All of these factors affect how they interact with and support your organization.

As an example, consider the March of Dimes. Its original mission was to eradicate polio, a disease much feared during the 20th century because of the paralysis and limb deformity it often produced in children. People born after the polio vaccine was developed didn't have the same fears and therefore were less inclined to support the March of Dimes. The nonprofit survived, however, after revising and expanding its child-focused mission to concentrate on prevention of birth defects.

TECHNOLOGY

What computer equipment, electronic gadgets, or digital devices are being tested or are on the drawing board? How might their use change how people communicate or interact? Addressing such questions opens up discussions on how your organization can better capitalize on the technology that's already available and prepare (and budget) for what's coming.

POLITICS

One state's decision to change a law related to fundraising activities or tax-exempt status can have serious repercussions across the country as other states follow suit. Likewise, valuable lessons can be learned from seeing how other nonprofits responded to a situation your organization may be facing in the regulatory or legislative arena.

FOR-PROFIT SECTOR

What happens within, to, and between corporations often has a trickle-down effect on nonprofits. When companies experience rapid growth, merge, or diversify, those developments tend to be reflected later in the nonprofit world. At the corporate level, everything has the potential to change the way nonprofits do business — from management trends to employee benefits, from communication vehicles to board policies.

In the 1990s, for instance, many small- and medium-sized companies disappeared as mergers and acquisitions reshaped the corporate landscape. This led to lower revenues for some nonprofits, as two or even three corporate donors or dues-paying members became one. In turn, nonprofits had to adjust their fundraising approaches and expectations and, in some cases, merge themselves to remain financially viable.

Another trend that picked up speed when the 21st century dawned was brand management. Companies, recognizing the equity in their product names, slogans, and packaging, began devoting more effort to strengthening their brands and thus their position in the marketplace. The same marketing principles are increasingly being applied to nonprofits to build name recognition, program participation, and financial support.

NONPROFIT SECTOR

What other nonprofits are doing also influences your organization, especially if you are competing for the same clients, customers, employees, donors, or supporters. By collecting benchmarking data, and by simply listening to the word on the street, you can pick up information that helps your organization stay competitive in numerous areas.

You have several options for tracking the trends that could reshape your organization. Some groups periodically invite a futurist to address their boards or ask a retreat facilitator to present a trends overview to set the stage for strategic planning. Others appoint a trend-analysis committee to scan various sources (books, articles, newspapers, and Web sites) and identify potential trends with long-term implications. Having such an early warning system in place enables the groups to have a strategy to prepare for and deal with change long before the crisis point is reached.

Not all trends identified by outside experts or your own stakeholders will come to pass. Other trends may have much greater effect than anticipated: Few people, even experts in the industry, predicted how computers would reshape international business and communications. And any unexpected, significant event — such as the terrorist attacks of September 11, 2001 — can have implications for years to come.

That's why your strategic plan needs to be flexible enough to accommodate growth, evolution, and outright transformation. As opportunities present themselves, your organization can reshape its products, benefits, and services accordingly, reinventing itself in the process.

Different, Yet the Same

Case in Point: National FFA Organization

Indianapolis, Indiana

Sixty years after its founding in 1928, Future Farmers of America (FFA) found itself at a crossroads. The agricultural land that had traditionally produced its members — high school students whose families raised livestock or grew crops — was increasingly being gobbled up by suburban subdivisions and shopping malls. Not only did fewer students come from agricultural backgrounds but also fewer were choosing farming as a career. Long term, the organization faced a losing battle against demographic shifts.

Rather than become obsolete, the nonprofit evolved into the National FFA Organization in 1988. Within six years, FFA had its first national president from an urban area (who was also its first African-American president). By 2002, about one out of four (27 percent) of FFA's 450,000-plus members lived in a rural area; one out of three (34 percent) had an urban or suburban address. And some of the largest, most cosmopolitan cities in the United States — including New York, Chicago, and Philadelphia — were home to FFA chapters.

To do this, FFA changed more than its name. During the 1990s, the organization expanded its role to encompass more than 300 careers in the science, business, and technology of agriculture. Its mission statement reads: "The National FFA Organization is dedicated to making a positive difference in the lives of young people by developing their potential for premier leadership, personal growth, and career success through agricultural education. Agricultural education prepares students for successful careers and a lifetime of informed choices in the global agriculture, food, fiber, and natural resources systems."

In other words, FFA is no longer just about winning a ribbon at the state fair for a prize animal, although that remains an opportunity for those who desire it. Instead, most students learn about and compete in events related to such areas as entrepreneurship, biotechnology, animal care, forestry, and natural resources management.

In its quest for a broader mission, FFA built on what it already had and learned to diversify. But it hung on to one item that has remained virtually unchanged over 50 years: Its trademark official jacket in blue corduroy, to be worn only by active members.

Suggested Action Steps

1. Every three to five years, revisit the organization's vision and mission statements and discuss any revisions that may make one or both of them more relevant to the current environment.

2. Consider implementing a brand identity program, based on board policy, to build and maintain recognition of your mission among stakeholders as well as the general public.

3. Develop an ongoing process for tracking the various demographic, economic, and environmental trends that the board should have to consider reshaping your organization.

3.

Maximizing Global Opportunities

Traditionally, our organization has maintained a national scope. Some of us, however, are concerned that we are missing out on opportunities to expand internationally. What factors should we consider?

If your organization has a Web site, you are probably operating internationally whether you know it or not. The explosion of Internet usage throughout the world has opened the floodgates of information, enabling someone in Europe, Africa, or Asia to easily learn more about a U.S. based organization — and vice versa. Time zones and geographical boundaries do not exist in cyberspace.

Plus, the growth of multinational companies that provide the same products and services in numerous countries and the fact that air travel has become commonplace have increased people's comfort level. No matter where they live, people often eat the same types of foods, watch the same movies, and wear similar clothing. They get the latest news by watching CNN or accessing the Web sites of other worldwide news organizations. What's foreign is no longer strange or unknown.

That said, moving an organization with a local, regional, or national scope to the international arena has numerous implications. Simply adding the words international or global to your organization's name and mission statement won't do the trick. A truly international organization operates with a global mindset and culture even if its stakeholders are primarily based in one country. It becomes second nature for such a group to take into account the worldwide implications of every decision made or every activity undertaken.

Key Considerations

Expanding into international activities may not be a logical extension of your organization's mission statement. In that case, the board should analyze whether the potential for operating internationally is even worth pursuing. Or, perhaps, the mission needs to be revisited and revised so the organization can better capitalize on the unmistakable trend toward globalization.

The direction to expand globally must not only come from the board but also enjoy its full support. Consider the following questions, which can help your board frame the do-we-or-don't-we discussion.

What Would the Organization and Its Stakeholders Gain?

If your organization already enjoys high market penetration, it's only natural to look to other countries where people might be eager to purchase your products and services, attend your meetings and shows, even pay dues or make contributions to support your efforts. Your organization may not have competitors in some geographic areas, positioning it as the sole provider of solutions to people's unmet needs.

More is at stake, however, than a bigger organizational bank account. You may have key constituents whose own businesses or organizations

Planning Steps

After your organization has decided to expand internationally in some way, shape, or form, develop a plan. You might want to work with a consultant experienced in international affairs or appoint a special committee of volunteers to take on the task. In either case, make sure to address these three key issues:

1. Determine your organization's objectives in going global, and support each objective with specific tactics. For instance, is your aim business development? Leadership development? A larger donor base? Meeting the needs of everyone who needs your services, no matter where a person lives? How do you intend to achieve these goals? Link the global plan to the organization's overall strategic plan so the two are in sync.

would benefit from an entree into international markets — you could pave the way for those unable to make headway on their own. Or you may represent people with a vested interest in how international standards and policies are set for various sectors of the economy.

International activity is not a one-way street. Don't forget what your organization may be able to learn from abroad when it comes to fundraising, influencing public policy, program development, leadership development, or community service. Initiatives that succeed in one country can, possibly with a few tweaks, prove just as effective somewhere else. Widening your perspective can enrich your organization's culture and operations.

Another potential gain comes in the form of recognition as a good global citizen. Many U.S.-based organizations have undertaken international programs aimed solely at helping people in need — of medical attention, food, clothing, books, shelter, and educational materials. Although they sometimes require delicate negotiations with foreign governments, these humanitarian efforts are typically well-received by all parties involved.

WHAT WOULD THE ORGANIZATION AND ITS STAKEHOLDERS LOSE?

As alluring as the promise of increased revenues can be, the old saying holds true: It takes money to make money. Devoting dollars to support

2. Assess the market potential, including competitors, size of overall market, and market share. This enables you to choose appropriate marketing and communication vehicles for targeted countries and audiences.

3. Develop financial projections. To be realistic, your calculations should include the higher costs of doing business abroad, including conversions to U.S. currency. With a strategic plan in hand, you'll be less likely to undertake an activity based on the whim of a board member or staff member or, conversely, to underfund an initiative that shows great promise. Just be aware that currency fluctuations and political instability in other countries can wreak havoc on even the best-laid plans. The board should revisit international goals regularly and assess the progress being made in view of the funds invested.

an international expansion will probably mean shifting money away from an established program (perhaps one near and dear to the hearts of your stakeholders).

Not spending the money, however, might lead to a loss of market share or a diminished reputation as a leader or authority in the field.

WHAT ARE THE STAFFING IMPLICATIONS?

Without a dedicated staff in place, an organization can begin exploring the international arena and even generating revenues by tapping new markets and audiences. For a global mindset to be integrated throughout the organization, however, the board must make a statement by issuing a policy that designates the position responsible.

At least one person must be dedicated to developing and implementing any international initiatives. Ideally, any employees in this area should have international management or marketing experience, speak a foreign language, and have received cultural awareness training.

Beyond that, other staff members or consultants to your organization will need to do some homework. If publications or products are mailed abroad, what are the costs and customs requirements? What special meals may be required if a U.S. meeting attracts international attendees? What financial procedures need to be put in place to accept credit cards or wire transfers from abroad? Survey staff on their fluency in other languages so you know where to turn if something gets lost in translation.

WHAT ARE THE GOVERNANCE IMPLICATIONS?

Just like their domestic counterparts, international stakeholders will want a voice within the organization. Including board members from other countries may require a bylaws amendment, not to mention adjustments in how the board communicates, when and how it meets, how board orientation is handled, what is expected of each member, and so forth. You'll also need to consider how to develop future leaders from afar and how to keep them involved in committee or task group activities.

WHAT LEGAL ISSUES MAY ARISE?

Many nonprofit organizations based in the United States enjoy tax-exempt status; they aren't required to pay taxes on revenue generated by activities related to their tax-exempt purpose. That's not necessarily the case elsewhere. In other countries, for instance, your organization may have to pay tax on electronic transactions, sales of products and services, meetings or conventions, membership dues, or even charitable contributions.

Intellectual property is an especially hot issue. Other countries don't take the same approach as the United States to protecting copyrights and trademarks. You may have little recourse if an organization based abroad helps itself to your Web-based content.

An attorney well-versed in international law can help you around any obstacles and offer advice on how to reduce tax burdens; refunds or exemptions may be in order if certain procedures are followed. Your attorney can also provide guidance on activities such as licensing a product or publication to a foreign organization or setting up an office abroad.

How Can Communication Challenges Be Overcome?

Some organizations conduct all their business in English. Given the widespread acceptance of English throughout the world, language may not present a large barrier. Much will depend upon the prevailing customs within your organization's field. Within some medical circles, for instance, English is the accepted language and therefore translations aren't necessary.

On the other hand, some international groups designate several official languages, perhaps Spanish and French in addition to English. The multilingual approach may be more welcoming yet presents another set of challenges, such as providing translation services at meetings, translating and reprinting publications and marketing materials, and redesigning your Web site to handle several languages.

What's more, variations occur within languages. Just as the English spoken in Australia differs from that spoken in the United States or England, translating a document into Spanish doesn't guarantee that someone in Mexico will understand it in the same way as someone in Spain. And, regardless of the language used, the jargon and acronyms so commonplace in nonprofit organizations will have to be avoided altogether.

You'll also need to consider which communication vehicles are most effective at reaching people abroad, and the answer may be different in each country. Some organizations opt to place all their publications online for access by members who live in places where mail service is slow or unreliable. But Internet usage is not pervasive in many countries, so your organization may need to rely on faxes or phone calls to do business across various time zones.

Who Might We Partner With?

Expanding your scope of operations across the Atlantic or Pacific doesn't necessarily mean flying solo. In fact, you might be able to make inroads faster, less expensively, or more effectively by aligning with other organizations that share your values but have a better understanding of cultural contexts.

For instance, you might outsource a particular function or service to a supplier in another country, co-sponsor activities with international affiliates or sister organizations, or enter into a partnership agreement with a for-profit or nonprofit entity. Before signing any collaboration agreement, do your homework on the potential partner to reduce the likelihood of unwanted surprises. If you plan to license your logo or content to a for-profit publisher, for instance, make sure the company doesn't have a history of repackaging or repositioning others' materials solely for its own profit.

Ways To Globalize

Small steps taken toward globalization can lead to a leap forward in your organization's name recognition, reputation, and overall value. Follow each of these steps one at a time, assessing each activity's results and its relevance to your organization's strategic plan:

- **Study similar organizations.** Identify other groups that have registered success with global initiatives and analyze their strategies.

- **Establish chapters or affiliates overseas.** This popular approach provides your organization with a local link in various communities. Typically, each chapter or affiliate operates autonomously while adhering to organizational guidelines (such as mission, code of ethics, use of trademarks or logos, financial reporting, and so forth).

- **Attend meetings with your international counterparts.** Look for ways your organizations can work together to address similar issues or interests.

- **Revise the governance structure to encourage wider participation.** Board meetings via audio or teleconference may make more sense for directors scattered across time zones, although state laws probably require at least one face-to-face meeting annually. Avoid having a token international representative on the board, perhaps by forming a supplemental group to advise on global matters. You might also develop regional groups around the world.

These may not have a governance role directly but can still serve as sounding boards and advisory councils to ensure the board hears and heeds international viewpoints.

- **Remove financial barriers to participation.** Hold online conferences or seminars so people don't have to pay for intercontinental travel. Another option is to offer scholarships or grants to attract international attendees to face-to-face meetings and conventions.

- **Open up opportunities for interaction.** Actively recruit international participants for an ongoing, electronic dialogue, whether it's through e-mail forums, regularly scheduled chat sessions, or your Web site. Invite speakers from other countries to address your meetings. Conduct e-mail interviews so you can include quotations from international readers in your publications. Such networking can help people stay attuned to trends and developments elsewhere that may be headed their way.

- **Establish a global databank.** Help your constituents or stakeholders, no matter where they live, access and understand the business practices, policies, customs, and laws in other countries.

- **Facilitate purchases.** Have books or memberships to sell? Make sure your Web site can handle e-commerce, including acceptance of foreign currency.

- **Sponsor a study mission abroad.** Meeting face to face with their counterparts in other countries will help your constituents better understand global challenges and opportunities.

OPERATING WITHOUT BORDERS

CASE IN POINT: SOCIETY FOR HUMAN RESOURCE MANAGEMENT

Alexandria, Virginia

In the early 1990s, the Society for Human Resource Management (SHRM) created the Institute for International Human Resources for human resource practitioners who either worked for a global company or had a special interest in learning more about the field. A few years later the institute was reconfigured as SHRM Global Forum, a membership program available only online and targeted to people living outside the United States. Soon the program was reporting double-digit growth and had expanded to include members in 70 countries.

To create SHRM Global Forum, the society first changed its bylaws to allow for the new membership category. It is open only to people with residency outside the United States and who hold membership in a local human resources association (if one exists in that country). The forum has its own board of directors, supported by a five-member global advisory committee.

Another decision was purely financial: Members living overseas would have access only to products and services available online, accessed via a special Web site. Previously, SHRM had found that the dues collected from international members did not begin to cover the considerable costs associated with distributing printed materials outside the United States. So SHRM's monthly magazine, which is mailed to U.S. members, is posted online for international members. The online content is presented in a no-frills fashion, so it uploads and downloads quickly and doesn't drive up the Internet charges incurred by international members. SHRM Global Forum members can also access benchmarking data on human resources practices in other countries or regions.

In addition, SHRM has

- established partnerships with human resources associations in other countries to facilitate the exchange of information

- taken on a worldwide leadership role by serving as secretariat (headquarters) of the World Federation of Personnel Management Associations

- helped other countries establish human resources associations which, in turn, can partner with SHRM

Suggested Action Steps

1. Schedule a brainstorming session for board members to discuss the implications of expanding into international markets or programs.

2. Appoint a task force of board and staff members to research what steps, either large or small, your organization can take toward globalization.

4.

Transforming Governance

We've put a lot of effort into rethinking our organization's mission and purpose. What might our board do to implement change internally to better align with the new realities?

After reviewing the reason your organization exists (mission), agreeing on what it aspires to see happen (vision), and figuring out how you'll fulfill your mission (strategic plan), you will undoubtedly reach the conclusion that something has to change. At the least, you'll identify areas in which the current operational structure needs to be tweaked. Or, you may conclude that what's currently in place simply can't support the organization in the direction it is now headed.

Widespread, wholesale change may be in order, and that can happen only from the top down. The board must take the lead role as a change agent and influence a transformation throughout the organization, not being afraid to use itself as an example of how the status quo can be improved upon.

Let's say your stakeholders want to see the organization become more responsive to them and more adaptable to the marketplace, which is increasingly international in scope. Is the current governance structure too cumbersome to accommodate those desires? Is your board structured to move quickly when needed and to exhibit flexibility in procedures and policies? What processes are in place to continually scan the external environment and, when necessary, position your organization to take the lead on an emerging issue or community concern?

The operational structure may need to change as well. Staff restructuring is clearly the chief executive's domain; he or she may request assistance from board members with relevant experience. Has your organization traditionally been monolithic, with each employee or department focusing only on assigned responsibilities and perhaps protecting the turf it took years to establish? Have people gotten so comfortable with the way it has always been done that they are sacrificing efficiency and productivity? The board of directors has the responsibility to ensure any changes support strategic directions and to approve an appropriate budget.

MAKING CHANGE

As you grapple with what change may look like for your organization, it's helpful to review overall trends in organizational development within the nonprofit sector. Several trends are discussed in this section.

MERGERS AND STRATEGIC ALLIANCES

From community-based human service agencies to metropolitan United Ways to regional Girl Scout councils, nonprofits at every level began to collaborate more in the mid-1990s. Motivating factors frequently included increased competition for charitable contributions and grants, along with increased operating costs (especially employee salaries and benefits). Surveying the economic landscape often leads boards to realize that it is futile to duplicate efforts when much can be gained by exploring partnership options with other nonprofits.

The governance implications may be negligible or significant. For instance, merging your nonprofit with another is likely to require delicate negotiation regarding the number (and election process) of board members. You may need to set up a rotation system for the first few years to ensure representatives of both groups have top leadership roles. But if several nonprofits band together to form a purchasing group or hire a legislative advocate, yet maintain independent operations, their boards have to agree but do not have to intertwine.

Smaller Boards

The bigger the board, the more unwieldy decision making tends to be. Members of large boards often don't feel connected to one another or even the organization, making them more likely to skip meetings and not fulfill their other responsibilities. They simply feel as if no one will notice their absence.

Some organizations have streamlined to the point of eliminating the executive committee entirely; having a smaller board (20 people or fewer) enables them to fully engage everyone in the work that used to be done by the top leaders. On the other hand, you don't want a board so small that members feel overwhelmed by all they have to do. Every organization will have its own ideal board size; research conducted by BoardSource indicates that the average nonprofit board of directors numbers 19 people.

When considering the downsizing option, use these questions to frame the discussion:

- What percentage of board members attend meetings regularly (more than 75 percent of the time)? Has this percentage gone up or down in recent years?

- Do board members feel comfortable engaging in discussions, or do they rubber stamp whatever staff present? (Larger boards tend to stifle discussion.)

- Is the board productive? Or is its size getting in the way of decision making?

- Do board members feel valued? Or do they express the feelings that they are superfluous and not really needed?

FEWER COMMITTEES

Unless your nonprofit is the exception, you've undoubtedly noticed that volunteers want to devote less time to attending meetings and engaging in busy work. When they are present, board members want to be useful. That means appointing them to committees that truly do board-level work instead of perpetuating a system of standing committees that may have outlived its purpose.

Board-appointed committees should deal with policies and strategies. Organizational committees, which do not necessarily need representation from the board, should focus on issues or concerns related to specific programs or service delivery. You probably don't want to eliminate your finance committee because it serves a key role in helping the board fulfill its fiscal responsibilities, and every board should have a governance committee to help steer board development. However, everything else should be open for debate.

So you'll have a better idea of how effective your current structure is, answer the following questions.

- How does each standing committee's purpose relate to our mission and goals?

- What benefit does this committee provide to the board and to the entire organization?

- Does this committee duplicate work done by staff?

Resist the temptation to create a committee for every new initiative or emerging issue. Instead, appoint a task force to oversee a special project (such as a capital campaign or bylaws review), then dissolve it upon completion of the project. Convening short-term task forces as the need arises not only makes board members feel needed but also restricts their time commitment.

FEWER MEETINGS

Again, volunteers feel pressed for time. They don't want to spend days attending a meeting on the other side of the country or even hours driving across town. Streamlining board governance often includes reducing the number of board meetings and making each meeting more efficient (through the use of consent agendas, the absence of routine committee reports, and a focus on policy rather than operational issues).

Some organizations keep the same number of meetings but don't always hold them face to face. For instance, the 12 members of one nonprofit's board meet only once a year in person; the other five board meetings are all conducted via audioconference. This enables the group, which doesn't have the funds to reimburse travel expenses, to attract board members from around the country.

GREATER EMPHASIS ON OUTCOMES

It's not enough to report to stakeholders that your organization is making progress on its goals. Increasingly, they want to see measurable results of that progress, which typically calls for development of an evaluation process for each program or area.

A MATRIX MENTALITY

A matrix has both a vertical and horizontal axis, enabling you to formulate numerous options and solutions. Organizations with a matrix mentality often organize cross-departmental teams, assembling the best people for each specific task regardless of their job titles. Hierarchy tends to diminish while flexibility increases.

Taking a tip from the for-profit sector, one nonprofit has reorganized volunteers and staff into teams that focus on a particular issue within the field. The teams are supported by a shared-services staff that handle such functions as clerical assistance, accounting, and human resources. The volunteers appointed to each team have a variety of skills and experience, whereas in the past the group tended to appoint committees whose members all had similar industry backgrounds or specialties.

This approach is in stark contrast to the silo mentality that often exists in nonprofits where volunteers or employees have carved out niches for themselves and seem reluctant to collaborate with others. It's also a trend that has prompted numerous organizations to move to an at-large governance mindset and eliminate board positions that represent a particular region or area. It then becomes the responsibility of the nominating committee to ensure the board as a whole accurately reflects organizational and geographic diversity.

TRANSPARENCY

Any moves you make toward reducing the number of volunteers involved in governance may be met with skepticism. Some stakeholders may express concern that changes will concentrate power in the hands of an elite few or that some grass-roots voices will be ignored. Others want to ensure that your organization remains open in all of its business dealings, even those involving board business.

Your response should be to communicate, again and again, how the changes will benefit the organization. Explain the new decision-making process, post a frequently asked questions (FAQ) page on your Web site, in your publications feature interviews with volunteers (not just the board chair) who are energized about the changes, host discussion groups with stakeholders, and so forth. Be open about every step you undertake, and invite people throughout the organization to join you on the journey.

Few organizations attempt transformation on their own. Involving an outside consultant or facilitator not only brings the necessary expertise and a fresh perspective to the situation but also can keep your organization on track. Without a consultant gently prodding the chief executive and board, it's easy to put off internal change to focus on continuing service to clients, customers, or members. That simply perpetuates the status quo. In addition, a consultant can help you figure out the best way to communicate changes to your stakeholders, particularly those that may require the approval of dues-paying members.

If your budget can't accommodate the cost of consulting fees, try to arrange for an expert to provide pro bono services.

UP FOR RENEWAL

No matter what governance changes have been made or are afoot, your board needs to do a regular self-check on how it's doing. Surprisingly, few nonprofit boards make the effort to assess their own performance even though they put a premium on evaluating everything else, from programs to financial results.

Most organizations that reshape their governance structures do so after reviewing results of a board self-evaluation. This short, confidential questionnaire asks board members to rate, usually on a numerical scale, how well the board does in various areas. You might want to ask such questions as the following:

- How clear is the organization's mission to you?

- How clear is your role on the board to you?

- How effective is the board's decision-making process?

- How effective is the board's strategic planning process?

- How productive are the board committees?

- Describe the quality of communication: among board members, between board and staff, from other stakeholders to board members, and so forth.

Invite written comments by including a lead-in phrase such as, "If I could change three things about how this board operates, they would be . . . . "

You'll end up with a candid summary of what the board does well and where it could stand improvement. For instance, the findings may point to board members' desire to make better use of their time, focus more on meaningful issues rather than administrative tasks, interact more with one another, or simply enjoy their positions more. The board as a whole should discuss the findings and what can be done to improve its effectiveness or productivity.

After completing a self-evaluation, one organization revamped agendas for board meetings to include three distinct parts: discussion of strategic issues by the whole board, business items, and a presentation by an outside expert who usually focuses on an important issue or emerging trend. The same group also cut in half the number of its standing committees and task forces so it could make decisions more spontaneously and invested in a password-protected Web site where board members could communicate between meetings.

The results of the self-evaluation, taken together with a new direction that may have emerged from the process of reviewing the mission and revising the strategic plan, can form the basis for a total transformation plan. Implementation of that plan, however, will require patience — talking about change is easier than making it happen. You may have some board members eager to get started right away, which can alienate those who are more cautious or want to do further research. Other stakeholders may not be psychologically or emotionally ready to bid goodbye to traditional practices and behavior patterns. On both the board and the staff, you'll need to line up change champions who can articulate not only what the changes entail but also the rationale behind them.

SMALLER AND SPEEDIER

CASE IN POINT: NATIONAL PTA

Chicago, Illinois

The 2,000 delegates attending the 2001 convention of the National PTA (Parent Teacher Association) had many decisions to make. On top of a proposed dues increase (for the second consecutive year), they had to consider the merits of changing the way the organization had made decisions for decades.

The proposed changes were substantial. They called for a significantly smaller board, a 62-percent reduction in the number of committees, and the creation of a new entity to be representative of (and more responsive to) the National PTA's 6.5 million members. Drafted by a task force charged with creating a more responsive governance structure, the changes aimed to make the nonprofit more competitive and nimble in the marketplace.

Other, newer organizations were moving into areas that the National PTA had long dominated. Members of its 87-member board (which at one time had numbered 109) were accustomed to making decisions at the state and local levels and brought that hands-on management mind-set with them; policy discussions often took a back seat while the board debated such operational issues as the color of business cards. All of this became clear to the board when it approved a new strategic plan in 1999 and subsequently created the governance task force. Then board members had to tackle the tough issue of essentially voting themselves out of a job by submitting the task force's recommendations to the convention. Throughout the process, the elected president and chief executive worked together to promote change and communicate the same message: If the National PTA didn't change, it might not survive.

After much discussion and deliberation, the delegates approved the bulk of the task force's proposal. Even with the amendments, the changes were sweeping. The National PTA now has a 28-member board and seven standing committees (instead of 16), plus the National Council of States, which is charged with "bringing issues, trends, and areas of concern to the national level."

To ensure the board remains representative of the organization, the National Council elects seven (25 percent) of the members and the nominating committee presents a slate of 10 member representatives for the board's approval. The 11 remaining board positions — three officers, two youth members, and six at-large members (from outside the PTA) — are appointed by the president and approved by the board.

Both volunteers and staff see a new role developing for board members. As they spend less time dealing with operational issues, board members will have more opportunities to engage in fundraising activities to support programs that ultimately benefit grass roots members.

Suggested Action Steps

1. Meet informally with board members from several other nonprofit organizations to discuss how and why they have recently revised their operational or governance structures.

2. Ask board members to complete a confidential survey with questions pertaining to their experience on the board, perceptions of the organization, and personal expectations.

3. Analyze benchmarking data and survey results with an eye toward streamlining, improving, or reforming the way the board and committees operate.

Part II

Finances

5.
Fiscal
Fitness

How can we ensure we remain in the best financial position possible, especially when the economy experiences fluctuations?

To determine your organization's level of financial fitness, you need to look at all related policies, practices, and procedures, in addition to investment strategies.

Chances are, the majority of your board members are not bankers, CPAs, or investment brokers, so a periodic review of the various pieces of the financial pie can help all of them fulfill their fiduciary responsibilities. Provide answers to the questions below and encourage other inquiries to clear up any confusion or misunderstandings board members may have about these areas.

ANNUAL OPERATING BUDGET

The annual operating budget document, typically developed by staff with volunteer input and board approval, outlines the organization's goals and activities for the year and attaches a price tag to each one. Balancing out the anticipated expenditures — and perhaps exceeding them — is expected income.

Some members who are new to the board may express surprise that the budget calls for a surplus rather than breaking even, as the term nonprofit may suggest. A board-level discussion might be in order, with the board chair or other leaders noting that nonprofits have the main goal of advancing a charitable, social, professional, humanitarian, or educational cause.

Yet, while nonprofits are not primarily in business to make a profit, they are not prohibited from doing so.

A nonprofit reinvests its profits in programs and operations that advance its mission, instead of paying profits to shareholders in the form of cash dividends as for-profits do. An end-of-the-year surplus for a nonprofit not only points to successful efforts by both staff and volunteers but also gives the organization something to invest for those years when the balance sheet tips the other way. Among the questions to consider are the following:

- Does the board regularly receive financial statements that include budget information? It's helpful for board members to compare actual expenses and revenues to those budgeted, including the percentage of variance. These statements should be reviewed at each board meeting so all board members remain aware of profit-and-loss performance.

- Who develops the budget each year? If volunteers have a role in budget development, they must receive the information needed to make realistic projections (such as prior-year performance or pricing trends within the field).

- What philosophy guides budget preparation? In one nonprofit, members of the finance committee agree in writing to cautiously project revenues and to generously project expenses. Another uses a simple rule of thumb: It overestimates expenses by 10 percent and underestimates income by 10 percent.

- What policies apply to budget revisions? How much flexibility does the staff have to reallocate income or expenses as the fiscal year unfolds? Many organizations do not allow budget revisions. Instead, they keep detailed notes on why a deviation occurred so future budget planners will have better information on hand. Requiring board approval on any significant revisions can be an effective internal control: Fraudulent activity or misuse of funds may come to light. Too, if a program does not meet revenue expectations and a shortfall is likely, the board can swiftly take corrective action, such as scaling back other programs or postponing some expenditures.

RESERVES

Reserves, also referred to as the fund balance, are the assets that remain after subtracting the organization's financial obligations as defined by the budget. Nonprofit organizations are generally advised to maintain reserves equal to between three and six months of their annual operating budget. In other words, an organization with a $600,000 annual budget would ideally have reserves of $300,000 in case a cash-flow emergency arose.

Strategic decisions will affect the level of reserves at any given time. An organization planning to buy a building may accumulate extensive reserves only to see the fund decrease dramatically after the purchase takes place. Whatever the reason for maintaining reserves, nonprofits should consider the following questions.

EXPERT ADVICE

Seeking outside assistance can lighten the burden of committee and staff members charged with making the most of the organization's money. Consider the following tactics when working with an investment advisor:

- **Choose an investment advisor with experience in the nonprofit sector.** Better yet, find someone who's managed portfolios of similar size. Check references to ensure that the advisor will follow your organization's investment guidelines regarding asset allocation and whether his or her investment personality (cautious versus speculative) is a good fit for your organization. Also find out with whom you would actually be working — the person who made the sales presentation or a customer service team?

- **Give the advisor some flexibility.** As part of the asset allocation guidelines, specify ranges for each class so your investment advisor has the authority to move some funds to take advantage of the market. You might, for instance, specify that between 15 to 25 percent be invested in mutual funds that specialize in companies without a large market value (small cap funds), with an equivalent range for large cap funds.

What Is the Reserve Policy?

Some stakeholders may take issue with earmarking money for reserves when it could be spent delivering the programs and services that remain the organization's reason for being. The board, guided by the finance committee and with an eye on the strategic plan, must balance short- and long-term objectives. For instance, a higher level of reserves may be warranted if the organization is contemplating new program initiatives (which carry higher financial risk) or a major purchase.

Your auditor can provide data on the reserve policies of similar nonprofits within the community. National associations and societies in your field often gather benchmarking data as well, which can be helpful for developing a policy and supporting rationale.

- **Review the investment fees assessed each year.** Are they reasonable and in line with what other organizations pay? Some groups pay a flat fee, while others pay a percentage of the value of their total assets. The latter approach, also known as fee for services, provides the advisor with an incentive to ensure investments perform well. Note that alternative investments — which include venture capital, hedge funds, and managed futures — tend to have higher management fees, as do real estate investments and international stocks and bonds. Don't hesitate to renegotiate fees, especially as the size of your organization's portfolio grows.

- **Periodically invite financial advisors and managers to provide education.** They should update the investment, finance, and executive committees on trends in the financial industry, specific market occurrences, and the pluses and minuses of various strategies. Just be sure the speaker can translate investment terms and jargon into plain English and is open to answering questions.

How Much of the Reserves Are Liquid?

The phrase *liquid reserves* refers to cash on hand and assets that can easily be converted to cash with little risk of loss (such as marketable securities). This is sometimes called the *operating reserve*.

Nonliquid reserves are those assets tied up in furniture, equipment, a headquarters office, other property, a for-profit subsidiary, or a related foundation. Converting them into cash not only takes longer but also carries a higher risk of loss. Nonliquid reserves might include restricted gifts that would otherwise be considered liquid. For instance, a donor may give $200,000 of stock to your organization with the restriction that it not be sold for a certain number of years.

What Are the Operating Ratios for Key Areas?

Determine what percentage of total expenditures goes to such areas as salaries and benefits, fundraising, publishing, and so forth. Also calculate the percentage of annual expenditures represented by additions to the reserves. Compare your ratios to those of similar organizations to get a better picture of how well you're doing (or what you could be doing better).

Being Prudent

Virtually all states have adopted the Uniform Prudent Investor Act, which governs how trustees may invest trust funds. Even if your nonprofit does not rely on income from a charitable trust, the act provides guidelines for deciding how funds should be invested.

The Prudent Investor Act states that trustees have a duty to

- diversify assets to minimize risk

- analyze investment decisions to ensure that the risks taken are appropriate to and compliant with the terms of the trust

- minimize fees, transaction costs, and other investment-related expenditures

WHAT ARE THE CASH-FLOW PROJECTIONS?

Looking ahead to when large expenditures are projected, the board needs to be aware of the potential for dipping into reserves. This often occurs when a headquarters building or other property is purchased or when programs are significantly expanded.

INVESTMENT FUNDS

Liquid reserves represent the funds available for investment. The reserve policy set by the board, taken together with the organization's cash flow, will guide the type of investments selected. Even the cash needed to cover day-to-day operations can be invested in some way, such as earning interest on a checking account and not paying invoices until they are due. Consider the following investment questions.

WHAT IS THE OPERATIONAL CYCLE?

Most organizations have high points and low points for revenue — a certain month or time of year when charitable contributions are received, a large program takes place, or dues are collected. If the organization's balance drops to zero right before the expected influx of revenue, it would need to quickly generate cash. That would point to the need for short-

- take into consideration factors such as the general state of the economy, likely effects of inflation (or deflation), and tax consequences of investment decisions

- delegate investment and management functions if desired, provided the trustees periodically review the investment manager's work

Where once trustees were prohibited from making certain types of imprudent investments, now they may consider investment options ranging from foreign securities and private equities to venture-capital hedge funds. The full portfolio is what has significance from a risk standpoint, as opposed to individual transactions.

term, low-risk investments such as Treasury bills and insured certificates of deposit.

Some organizations maintain a sweep account that's equivalent to two or three weeks of day-to-day operations. The organization earns investment income on the account and has access to it each day; whatever is not spent is automatically reinvested.

DOES THE ANNUAL BUDGET DEPEND ON INVESTMENT INTEREST OR DIVIDENDS?

The financial markets are too fickle to rely on investment returns as part of projected revenues, unless the organization has money market or certificates of deposit accounts exclusively. Warning bells should sound in board members' ears if the proposed operating budget includes income from investment portfolios that contain equity holdings. (The exception would be a foundation that typically spends a set percentage of its assets each year.)

INVESTMENT GUIDELINES

Board members undoubtedly think long and hard about their personal investment choices. Asking them to also make or manage investment choices on behalf of the organization may be asking too much.

If the size and diversity of your investments merit it, consider appointing an investment committee to handle much of the detailed analysis of investment choices and to make recommendations for the board to review and approve. With members well-versed in money management, the investment committee can come up with policies and a strategy that meet the organization's current needs while reflecting economic trends such as inflation, consumer spending, and interest rates. An investment strategy adopted when a nonprofit is in a growth phase, trying to build reserves, will differ from that set when the group is more focused on preserving its reserves and generating income. Because needs change as the organization evolves, the committee should revisit its policies annually.

Financial decisions made on behalf of a nonprofit organization should be thoughtful and well-informed. Committee members must analyze each option presented by staff or financial advisors in terms of the degree of risk involved, the investment yield, and the ability to access the funds (liquidity). In general, the lower the risk, the greater the liquidity (think of a savings account that pays low interest but allows for withdrawal of funds at any time). An investment vehicle promising a higher yield also carries a higher risk (junk bonds, for example).

Most nonprofit organizations take a conservative approach and aim for a mix of low-risk, short-term investments (those that mature within one to five years, such as mutual funds) and higher-risk, long-term investments (stocks and bonds held for three to five years). In recent years, some nonprofits have gotten more aggressive and adopted policies that allow them to invest in hedge funds and venture-capital deals.

Investment guidelines generally cover

- the organization's overall investment philosophy. This guides decisions for the long term, making organizations more likely to stay the course during turbulent economic times rather than panic and pull out all assets. One organization, for instance, abides by a 60:40 philosophy: 60 percent in equities (mostly value stocks) and 40 percent in fixed assets

- the kinds of investments allowed or prohibited (risk)

- how investments should be allocated (liquidity). What percent should stocks represent? What percent should be allocated to bonds? Provide the rationale for each class of assets selected and how, taken together, they offer balance and diversity

- how performance will be measured (yield). At a minimum, this measurement should be done quarterly. Decide what index to use as a performance benchmark, such as the Standard & Poors 500

- how often, and in what format, reports will be given to the board

Incidentally, the investment committee is one place where you don't want to see a lot of turnover from one year to the next. People need time to understand the organization's investment strategy and financial culture. For continuity and a commitment to long-term results, try to add only one new member every two years or so. Just guard against keeping the same membership in place for so long that inertia sets in. The organization's investment philosophy and policies must be revisited frequently and revised to accommodate economic fluctuations as well as changes or developments in mission-related activities.

When investments do not perform as expected or hoped, take a look at the economic environment as a whole before making any sweeping changes. After the collapse of the dot-com economy in 2001, which was followed by a more severe economic downturn after the terrorist attacks of September 11, 2001, many nonprofits saw the value of their investments plummet and charitable contributions decrease. The prevailing response was not to greatly alter investment strategies but rather to look at the operational budget for ways to cut costs, increase dues or fees, emphasize marketing of products and services, and increase membership or attendance.

Suggested Action Steps

1. Periodically devote part of a board meeting to financial education; ask outside experts or board members serving on the finance committee to review financial policies and budgetary procedures.

2. Invite a representative from the investment committee or your investment management firm to update board members on the organization's current investment philosophy and invite their feedback.

3. Consider a board briefing by an outside investment advisor who has experience in the nonprofit sector; then evaluate the pros and cons of depending on that or another advisor rather than having board members managing investments.

6.

Investing in Technology

Just a few years ago, we invested in a new information technology system, and it's already out of date. How can we afford to keep up with technological advances?

Every day seems to bring news of another technological development that promises to transform the way people communicate, socialize, relax, work, and conduct business. Purchase a system one week — after carefully budgeting for it a year in advance — and the next week you might already feel behind the times. It then becomes tempting to purchase bits and pieces of technological solutions that don't necessarily go together or achieve the intended effect.

What can technology potentially do for your organization? In considering that question, the board of directors can better determine how high a priority technology needs to be and budget accordingly every year. As with any other aspect of nonprofit operations, technology takes resources, and the level of funding should reflect organizational strategy.

The board may decide the organization does not have to be on the cutting edge of technology but still needs to remain productive and competitive without investing in unproven technologies. Or the board may have a policy that technology is the driving force behind every activity undertaken. For example, one nonprofit that represents information technology professionals spends heavily on technology because its mission includes advancing the profession itself. The group prints no publications and holds few face-to-face meetings, but members can access numerous products and services and network with one another via sophisticated Internet tools and a Web site that's updated frequently.

A Strategic Approach

Let's face it, computers and the Internet are here to stay, and their wide-spread use is reshaping operations of for-profits and nonprofits alike. A nonprofit still in the start-up phase may have no other choice than to beg and borrow various pieces of office equipment and cobble together a computer system. Beyond that, however, you need a formal technology plan, developed by staff, to address the organization's ongoing and evolving needs.

Without a plan in place, you'll never feel as if you have caught up with what the rest of the world is doing with and through technology. Information technology isn't something an organization can deal with once every two or three years and then forget about. It needs to be an integral part of every discussion, not simply tacked onto a proposed budget or a new program initiative.

Just like the overall strategic plan that guides everything an organization does, a technology plan outlines short- and long-term goals and then addresses the specific steps toward those goals. In fact, the technology plan should use your organization's mission and purpose as its starting point: What do you want to accomplish? How can technology facilitate that? By focusing more on the ends and less on the means, you're less likely to get caught up in the technology itself and more apt to see its many possibilities.

Below are the recommended steps to take toward developing a workable plan.

Step 1: Establish a Technology Team

An information technology system is a nuts-and-bolts operational item and therefore is the chief executive's responsibility. Yet the board has a duty to develop organizational strategies, which will influence what type of system is needed. The board, for instance, may charge the chief executive with appointing a six- to eight-member team that includes employees in various areas and possibly volunteers, including board members with the technical expertise and a willingness to give extra time beyond their board responsibilities.

To assist the team, the chief executive may call in an outside consultant who specializes in technology planning and support. This person can ask thought-provoking questions and help keep the team on track as it evaluates the organization's current technology infrastructure and decides how to transform it.

CAPITALIZING ON TECHNOLOGY

No doubt about it, technological tools can be expensive. They can also boost efficiency and expand revenues and services, providing a significant return on investment. Nonprofits are using technology to cut costs, improve productivity, connect with stakeholders, and enhance the bottom line by using

- **Virtual communities.** Your organization can connect with people online no matter where they live. Through online chats, discussion boards, and e-mail forums, you can stay in touch with donors or other constituents who may have moved away from your service area but still want to feel a part of the organization.

- **Electronic board books.** The large mailing envelope, stuffed with minutes, financial reports, and committee updates can be a thing of the past. One group has lightened the load on its three-person staff (and reduced copying and postage costs) by establishing a board home page on its Web site. Board members download and review the relevant documents on their own schedule and can post messages in a board-only area between meetings.

- **Intranets.** These internal networks, for employees only, offer an efficient means of communicating information and sharing documents.

- **Online fundraising.** Research suggests that the average gift made online is more than 20 percent higher than that made via a direct mail appeal. You'll have to pay a fee for each credit-card transaction, but that may be balanced by the staff costs associated with manually processing checks. Before using the Internet to raise funds, however, develop a privacy policy to assure donors you will not share their information outside of your organization. Also take steps to offer a secure online connection to guard against the theft of credit-card numbers.

- **Online registrations.** This is not only convenient for people wanting to attend an event but also can save staff time — once information has been entered electronically into your organization's database, via your Web site, it doesn't need to be reentered. Again, ensure you have safeguards in place to protect people's credit card numbers.

- **E-commerce.** Any product or service your organization promotes through traditional means, such as direct mail, advertising, press releases, and catalogs, can be featured online as well. People can purchase products 24 hours a day, seven days a week, not just when your customer service staff is available. Some services, such as classified advertising and find-a-vendor programs, can also be available around-the-clock.

- **Online surveys.** Although their statistical validity is sometimes questionable, Web-based surveys can provide snapshots of what your stakeholders are thinking and doing. That qualitative input can be helpful when a quick decision is needed. Plus, surveys are an effective means of gathering information on visitors to your Web site so you can tailor content accordingly.

- **E-mail newsletters.** Many organizations use these to promote programs or alert constituents to developing issues. Others have taken the next step and use customized e-mail newsletters to drive people to their Web sites, often including links to content specifically selected to match the recipient's interests. E-mail newsletters usually work well in combination with other electronic initiatives, such as asking people to complete an online survey or register for an event. One university sends a biweekly e-newsletter to all alumni who opt in (request it) and always includes a link to a secure online giving page. Contributions consistently spike within 24 hours of each e-newsletter transmission.

- **Downloadable documents.** Some nonprofits have cut down their printing costs by storing forms, standards, and other copy-intensive documents on the Web sites. Visitors can download portable document format (pdf) versions of the materials, for free or for a fee, and print the materials themselves.

- **Web seminars.** Follow the lead of colleges and universities that offer classrooms in cyberspace; no matter where students are located, they can access a course's Web site and participate via e-mail and online discussions.

- **Online voting.** Most states have not yet adopted statues that permit nonprofit membership organizations to conduct board elections via the Internet. That time will come, however, so you can prepare now by revising your bylaws. Depending on the state, however, some board business can be conducted online.

Even after a technology plan is finalized, it requires revisions and fine-tuning to accurately reflect technological as well as organizational developments. For instance, has your organization decided to cultivate stakeholders in other countries? Then you'll need a database that can accommodate foreign addresses. The team or committee should continue to meet periodically to evaluate progress and address short-term concerns as they arise.

Step 2: Conduct an Audit

If you have not recently conducted an organizational assessment, take the time to consider how you actually get things done. What structures, systems, products, and services are in place? How and when do you communicate with key audiences? What type of information do you disseminate? In what areas does the organization excel — and where can it do better?

Reaching Outside

As your technology plan develops, team members may reach the conclusion that your organization does not have the in-house expertise or the infrastructure to match its priorities. The good news is you don't have to do it all yourself. Outsourcing functions to a technology vendor can give you access to the latest and greatest tools available without having to make a capital investment. Plus, an outside vendor can get your organization up to speed quickly, which may be an important consideration. Web site hosting, database maintenance, and e-commerce fulfillment are just some of the functions that nonprofits often outsource.

When you look for a technology partner, keep the following in mind:

- **Ask about the company's experience in the nonprofit sector.** Better yet, ask about its experience in your field or industry. Ideally, you want to work with someone who is already up to speed on how nonprofits operate but will customize a solution for your organization rather than taking a one-size-fits-all approach. Look for a good fit between your organization and the company's culture.

- **Investigate the company's financial health.** How long has it been in business? Does it have sound financial backing? If the deal offered sounds too good (inexpensive) to be true, you could be headed for a

A traditional SWOT analysis (strengths, weaknesses, opportunities, and threats), typically done as part of an overall strategic planning process, can provide valuable results. In reviewing the results, the technology team will see some areas that require further examination — and perhaps retooling — and other areas where current practices are top-notch.

Note that this step does not focus specifically on technology but rather on the entire organization. That wider perspective is necessary for technology to truly be integrated into how the organization conducts its business.

STEP 3: CONSULT STAKEHOLDERS

Once the team has determined what the organization actually does, it must find out what the organization could do. Activities may include conducting written surveys, focus groups, and one-on-one interviews with representatives of your various constituencies. Ask staff what could

---

crisis. More than one nonprofit has seen its Web site crash when the firm hosting it declared bankruptcy and shut its doors without warning.

- **Find out who would do the actual work for your organization.** Arrange a meeting between the company's service representative(s) and your staff liaison.

- **Check references thoroughly.** Ask other organizations about the vendor's expertise in designing, customizing, and maintaining the system.

- **Develop written requirements.** Articulate what you want to achieve through the outsourcing arrangement. Perhaps your objective is to enhance and expand e-commerce on your Web site. Develop schedules for posting updates and new product information, specifying a 24- or 48-hour turnaround on orders placed.

- **Maintain control of content.** Even if your technology partner develops content or copy, make sure you own the rights and have final approval. This ensures that all interactions or communications with your stakeholders will reflect your organization's image and reputation.

- **Involve your attorney.** Consult with legal counsel as negotiations progress and a contract is developed. Don't sign anything until your attorney has reviewed — and probably revised — the company's standard terms. Make sure the contract includes a termination clause.

make their jobs more efficient or productive; inquire of donors, board members, and grassroots volunteers how they would like to communicate with you; question clients or customers about ways to meet their needs better. Find out everyone's comfort level with technology, particularly how (and how often) they use it in their personal life.

Although some answers will directly relate to technology ("Please buy a faster computer for me."), you're bound to hear broader observations as well. For instance, clients may say, "It sure would be nice if I didn't have to repeat the same information five times before finding the right person to talk to." The team will have to translate that into a potential technological solution, such as installing a customer relationship management (CRM) system or a unified communications (UC) system.

STEP 4: REQUEST PERIODIC UPDATES

Based on its research and observations, the technology team will zero in on the areas where the organization could better serve its stakeholders more effectively and efficiently. Ask staff to periodically review the resulting list of technology objectives at board meetings and to discuss how other nonprofits may be employing technology to improve operations.

Insist on a cost-benefit analysis for any proposed investment in technology. Make sure the investments support the stated objectives, rather than letting the availability of technological tools drive what you decide to do and when. The number of items on the team's wish list will undoubtedly outnumber the resources currently available, so identifying the most critical items and a phase-in plan will facilitate decision making at the board level.

Be sure to look a few years ahead: The organization's strategic plan may have an initiative two or three years out that would benefit from having a technology infrastructure already in place. Suppose you're planning a capital campaign, the first for your organization in 15 or 20 years. Computerizing old donor records and building a new database of potential contributors in advance will streamline operations once the campaign is launched.

STEP 5: PLAN LONG-TERM BUDGETS AND TIMELINES

After conducting in-depth research on the technological tools available and their potential costs, staff should inventory what is already on hand and what is needed to bring the technology plan to fruition. Then they can educate the board on how much it will cost — and how much time it will take — to fill the gaps. In addition to the equipment itself, staff should calculate the costs of software, training, and ongoing operation and maintenance. Vendors can help fill in many of the blanks by responding to a Request for Proposal that outlines various pieces of the technology plan. Talking with vendors and other organizations can help the team develop timetables that are realistic (although many organizations then add another 10 or 15 percent contingency time because technology projects typically take longer than expected).

Match your technological timelines to the strategic planning and budgeting cycles, usually between three and five years. Of course you can revise the plan along the way, but having a road map in hand keeps detours to a minimum. One organization, for instance, has a three-year technology plan that aligns with its annual budget preparation. Year 1 includes replacement of hardware, Year 2 focuses on replacing or upgrading software, and Year 3 is the time for investing in upgrades to the network. The cycle then starts all over again, enabling the group to depreciate the hardware over three years.

Another organization uses a rotation strategy that assumes no upgrades: Every year or two, the people needing the newest, fastest computers purchase them and hand their previous models down the line. A graphic designer working with digital video or Web site design, for instance, would need the most powerful computer, followed by production staff handling page layouts, followed by administrative and clerical staff who primarily need word-processing and Internet capabilities. That approach enables the group to invest in cutting-edge technology in the areas where it will provide the most benefit.

STEP 6: BEGIN IMPLEMENTATION

Before launching a new system across the organization, start with a pilot project in one or two departments. Then you'll have time to work out any kinks and, based on the staff and volunteer response, possibly revise your schedule for a full-scale introduction. You might discover that more in-depth training is needed before people feel comfortable with the technology or more marketing is needed to acquaint stakeholders with your new capabilities. What you learn may, in turn, affect future budgets.

STEP 7: EVALUATE YOUR PROGRESS

Go back to your stakeholders periodically and find out how well the technology plan is working. Has the organization become more productive, more efficient, better at communicating, better at customer service? The board needs to hear these results.

The technology team should meet at least once a year to review the evaluations and conduct a brainstorming session to identify emerging needs. By keeping the technology plan updated, your organization won't feel as if it is wasting money but rather investing it wisely, for a purpose.

Drumming Up Support

Case in Point: American Society of Anesthesiologists

Park Ridge, Illinois

When a proposed regulation or legislation has the power to make or break your organization, technology can be a powerful tool for educating constituents and spurring them to action. In particular, the Internet enables you to interact with many people at once yet communicate consistent messages to each one.

In 2000, facing the prospect of a Medicare rule that would have been detrimental to its members, the American Society of Anesthesiologists (ASA) invested in a technological approach to political advocacy. The educational, research, and scientific association of physicians hired a consulting firm to develop a special Web site where visitors could review news stories about the issue, download results of a relevant study, and sign up to receive free e-mail updates. They could also click on a link to send a message to the government agency developing the regulation.

ASA purchased banner and pop-up ads from a major Internet service provider and posted messages on various online lists targeted at senior citizens and the medical profession. All the promotional materials invited interested parties to visit ASA's Web site, and thousands did. Over the course of two years, about 70,000 people registered on the Web site and took some type of action, such as writing letters to their elected officials or providing the names of local media representatives. ASA's site was designed to capture such information as visitors' ZIP codes, enabling the society to identify and follow up with those in key states and congressional districts.

The campaign, the group's first foray into online advocacy, paid off when the Medicare ruling was amended to reflect ASA's position.

Suggested Action Steps

1. Establish a board policy requiring the staff to have a technology plan that outlines short- and long-term goals.

2. Appoint a task force of board, staff, and outside experts to analyze how the organization can make better use of technology to save time and money.

3. To control costs and take advantage of cutting-edge develop-ments, consider outsourcing some functions to a technology vendor with access to the latest tools or finding another nonprofit to share costs.

7.

Social

Entrepreneurship

As we evaluate our current programs and look toward the future, the term social entrepreneurship is entering more and more conversations. What is it, and what do we need to know about it?

Social entrepreneurship refers to a philosophy of self-sufficiency. It involves finding ways to generate revenue to be used to improve society, such as furthering a nonprofit's mission. Making a profit isn't so much the intent as effecting change in order to do good or make the world a better place. Any commercial or business venture undertaken should support or advance the main reason the organization exists.

The for-profit business literature is packed with examples of men and women who were willing to gamble — often everything they owned — on a new venture that eventually captured market share and generated significant profits. These entrepreneurs, who often work outside the existing system, rose to greater prominence in the mid-1980s and throughout the 1990s as well-established companies looked for ways to inject fresh ideas and creativity into their operations in order to develop new revenue streams.

What qualities come to mind when you hear someone described as being an entrepreneur? Perhaps *bold, creative, adventurous, willing to take a chance*, and *quick to capitalize on a new idea, among others*. Fostering an entrepreneurial spirit within the corporate environment became an economic necessity and, like most trends in the for-profit sector, it has filtered down to nonprofits.

The timing couldn't be better. Nonprofits are experiencing a reduction in the federal funds available to do their work and increased competition for financial support from individual donors and foundations. Everyone wants a piece of the pie, but there is only so much pie to go around. Social entrepreneurship, however, focuses on *creating* wealth, not simply redistributing someone else's money as nonprofits have traditionally done.

MANY POSSIBILITIES

Although the term may be new to you, the concept of social entrepreneurship is not necessarily new to nonprofits. As an example, Goodwill Industries International Inc., now headquartered in Bethesda, Maryland, was founded in Boston by a Methodist minister. He asked wealthy people to donate clothes, then hired immigrants to work at repairing and selling the clothes at the first Goodwill store. The year was 1902, and the minister's idea of combining work, job training, and assistance to low-income residents was referred to, in the terms of the times, as industrial evangelism. Thrift store sales now represent about one-half of Goodwill Industries International's revenues.

Or consider the P.E.O. Sisterhood, a philanthropic and educational organization based in Des Moines, Iowa. Since 1927, this nonprofit has owned and operated a two-year liberal-arts college for women — a gift from one of its 250,000 members — as part of its mission to "bring to women increased opportunities for higher education."

Many of the tools and perhaps even the infrastructure your organization needs to become a social entrepreneur may already be on hand (or, like the gift of the college, may suddenly fall into your lap). It's just a question of recognizing the potential for profit and then being willing to take the risk to do something differently.

In Kansas City, Missouri, the Don Bosco Community Center leveraged its existing facilities and expertise to launch a catering service. Known as the International Dining Experience, the service draws on the knowledge of the center's diverse staff to offer menus from Mexico, Pakistan, Somalia, and other countries. Most catered events fall on weekends and evenings, times when Don Bosco is not preparing meals for homebound senior citizens and those living in its senior center. Profits from the catering service are used to support Don Bosco's other community-based programs, including a nationalities service center (refugee resettlement, job placement, and immigration services), a family support center (food bank, clothes closet, and furniture warehouse), and a counseling center.

Share Our Strength, a Washington, D.C.–based nonprofit that works to eradicate hunger, profits from the brand equity it has built by licensing its organizational logo to food companies. When it licensed to a cookware manufacturer the logo of its Taste of the Nation events, Share Our Strength not only received royalties but also had the opportunity to educate consumers about hunger and poverty by providing copy for the cookware's packaging.

Minnesota Public Radio (MPR) in St. Paul, Minn., discovered it had a valuable asset in its loyal audience following. It formed a direct-mail catalog company named Rivertown Trading to sell products related to its radio programs, then branched out to offer other items that often had a nostalgic appeal for customers. Formed in the late 1980s, Rivertown Trading pumped an average of $4 million into radio programming annually. When the catalog company was sold to a department store corporation, the sale produced a permanent endowment for MPR of approximately $100 million, undoubtedly far more than the organization could have realized through traditional fundraising activities during the same period of time. (See Chapter 8 for more information on for-profit subsidiaries.)

PULLING IT ALL TOGETHER

All the information gathered during the feasibility phase can be reformulated as a business plan. This document doesn't have to be complicated but it should be detailed enough to address the questions and concerns likely to be raised by other board members and potential funders.

A business plan typically includes these five components:

1. **Summary of the Business.** This section should be brief, no more than two or three pages, and include descriptions of your organization and the new venture, an explanation of how the two are tied together, and key details on how the venture would be operated, who would be in charge, and where funding would come from.

2. **Overview of the Marketplace.** A detailed description of the proposed venture should cover what products or services you will provide to which target audiences. Discuss how the venture fits into the competitive landscape, including any unique characteristics that will set it apart.

Such innovation is sometimes publicly questioned or downright criticized. Some people automatically jump to the conclusion that a nonprofit — created primarily to do good — must be doing something wrong by making a profit. Yet they applaud corporations — which are primarily in business to make a profit — that act as good citizens and do something good. Although this attitude is changing, nonprofits should consider the public's perception of entrepreneurial activities. When the sale of Rivertown Trading was announced, for instance, MPR experienced a rash of negative media coverage and even attracted the attention of state regulators. The story quickly died when it became clear MPR had met all legal requirements in setting up and operating its catalog company.

LAYING THE FOUNDATION

Engaging in social entrepreneurship represents a significant cultural change for most organizations. Having spent decades making itself attractive to donors and grantmakers and squeezing the most out of scarce resources, a nonprofit may have to start devoting staff and money

3. **Staff Structure.** Include the name and title of the person who will oversee the endeavor, any new positions that need to be created, and the internal reporting relationships.

4. **Timetable for Implementation.** This involves a schedule for getting the new venture off the ground, which may include a pilot project plus steps to take before the actual opening of the business (preparing facilities, hiring staff, and so forth), and marketing strategies to attract and retain customers.

5. **Finances.** This overview of the venture's revenue potential should include the projected budget (ideally, covering the first three years), possible funding sources, and the funds that must be expended at each implementation step. Include worst-case and best-case scenarios so board members understand the financial continuum that applies.

to building and promoting a new service geared toward generating revenues. That's not to say development activities have to be curtailed, but a reordering of priorities may be in order.

Unless your organization was specifically founded with the intent of being self-sufficient, you'll need to prepare volunteers and staff for a foray into market-based activities.

REVIEW THE FINANCES

Are you in a position of strength, with adequate reserves, healthy cash flow, and a profitable bottom line? If not, launching a new venture is risky business. A nonprofit can't afford to do everything, so consider the trade-offs. If you focus on an entrepreneurial activity where you have the competitive advantage, you may need to cut back on activities in which you are not the market leader. At a minimum, assume that two years will pass before the venture breaks even and begins generating revenue.

ASSESS THE CULTURE

Do you have a history of being innovative and flexible, or would most people characterize your organization as traditional, careful, and conservative? Social entrepreneurship can succeed in risk-averse organizations, but you'll need to take more time to persuade stakeholders that they should support the idea. Staff, board members, and contributors alike need to understand how the venture complements or builds upon the mission.

Only after achieving buy-in internally can you successfully make your case in the marketplace. The organizational culture may be in transition, following a significant change in elected leaders or an influx of new senior staff. Even if those new people have an entrepreneurial bent, let them settle in before launching a new initiative. Social entrepreneurship requires energy and personal commitment, which can be in short supply when an organization is getting back on its feet after a crisis occurs, a new chief executive comes on board, or widespread change has rippled through its structure.

RECRUIT ENTREPRENEURIAL BOARD MEMBERS

No matter how visionary the chief executive, no matter how detailed the business plan, social entrepreneurship will fail if the board is not behind the idea 100 percent. Work with the nominating committee to recruit two or three people who are not only willing to take business risks but also have skills that might benefit a start-up venture, such as expertise in marketing, information technology, retail sales, or programming. Just be sure these entrepreneurial-minded members are comfortable with the group process that characterizes nonprofits. Select one board member to work closely with the chief executive in championing social entrepreneurship. He or she should be an informed, enthusiastic proponent who feels comfortable talking up the idea with other board members, staff, and stakeholders.

You may identify several potential candidates who aren't available to serve on the board. Be sure to keep their names and approach them later about possibly serving on a business advisory council or kitchen cabinet related to the social enterprise; a shorter-term, more focused commitment may be more appealing to them than board service.

DETERMINING FEASIBILITY

Once the foundation is in place, build upon it with pieces of information gathered through focus groups, conversations with community leaders, Internet research, written and oral surveys, and other forms of market research. Ideally, devote at least one year to amassing all the information that board members will need to make an informed decision. (That time frame may be a luxury you can't afford if you wish to capitalize on a market-driven opportunity. In that case, you'll need to condense the timetable but still complete all steps.)

Your first step in the feasibility phase should be to appoint a business ventures task group, consisting of staff, board members, and other stakeholders. Through qualitative and quantitative market research and trends analysis, this group should make determinations based on the issues described in this section.

ESTABLISH BENCHMARKS

Find out what other nonprofits are doing in your community and across the nation. What can you learn from their missteps and successes? Also scrutinize any entrepreneurial efforts your organization undertook in the past, whether or not they succeeded. With the perspective of time, you can more easily identify the weaknesses (Too little research? Not enough staff? Inability to adapt to changes in the marketplace?) and consciously avoid repeating them.

EVALUATE VENTURES AGAINST THE MISSION

Determine the appropriateness of potential ventures. Brainstorm the possibilities, always with an eye on the organization's mission. What does your organization do best? How might you build upon that expertise as well as the support of clients, members, and funders? What unmet needs are evident within your community or clientele? What entrepreneurial paths do you not want to go down, for fear of alienating stakeholders who are committed to the reason the organization exists? What external trends might you capitalize on to advance your mission? What activity might be a natural extension of something you're already doing?

Over the years, for example, the Dodge Nature Center (DNC) in West St. Paul, Minnesota, has pursued ventures that build upon one another and its overall mission "to provide nature-based education for children, families, and schools." The 320-acre, nonprofit nature preserve made its first move into social entrepreneurship in 1988 with the opening of a shop to sell birdseed, snowshoes, binoculars, and other nature-related items. In 1993, recognizing the prevalence of working mothers in the

WEIGHING THE PROS AND CONS

Here's how social entrepreneurship might help your organization:

- Pay for expense areas not traditionally covered by fund development activities, such as administrative and overhead costs.

- Diversify income sources to reduce reliance on a signature activity or big event, which could be easily affected by weather, timing, or competing activities.

- Raise your visibility within the community by providing another avenue for media coverage and another way for people to become connected to your organization.

- Build upon your mission by providing job training or employment to your target constituents.

community, it collaborated with the local school district to develop a full-day summer camp for children, later adding after-school programming during the school year. By 1999, DNC had launched a preschool, which, because of its unique environmental curriculum, charges tuition above market rate and still has a waiting list. And when its buildings are not in use by children, DNC rents conference rooms and classrooms to corporations hosting seminars or banquets.

ASSESS THE COMPETITION

Narrow the list to a handful of ventures and take a hard look at the marketplace. Who else provides the same service or product or serves the same market niche? What are your would-be competitors' strengths and weaknesses? What are prevailing standards within the market segment that you'll have to meet or exceed? If you plan to offer commercial foodservice, for example, what health codes must you comply with? If you want to open a print shop, what trade customs must you observe?

Consider the ripple effects of going head-to-head with an established business: To truly compete, you'll need to offer competitive salaries and

---

On the other hand, consider the potential drawbacks to an income-producing venture:

- Failure is an option. Every entrepreneur understands there are risks inherent in trying something new. The marketplace is simply too unpredictable to guarantee success, even with a solid business plan in place.

- The organizational structure and decision-making processes may not be flexible enough to accommodate a profit-oriented venture. Staff must be unencumbered by other duties and have the authority to make quick decisions that respond to marketplace demands.

- Unfavorable publicity may come your way, especially if you go head-to-head with for-profit competitors that see your nonprofit status as an unfair advantage.

- Stakeholders may become confused about the mission and overall values, express fear about the organization losing its soul in pursuit of profits, and even question their own continued support.

benefits to staff and invest in marketing efforts. One nonprofit even decided to pay the board members of its for-profit subsidiary, assuming that the corporate world would have paid them as well.

IDENTIFY POTENTIAL FUNDERS

Some organizations self-finance a social enterprise by drawing on their reserves or redirecting funds from another activity. Others take a pure business approach and obtain traditional bank financing, usually using reserves or building equity as collateral.

Externally, there may be more sources available than you might imagine, thanks to the growth of venture philanthropy — funders that provide technical assistance or consulting, as well as dollars, to assist nonprofits with ventures that have a promise of sustainability for the long term. Such funding typically comes with specific conditions the nonprofit must meet.

In the case of Don Bosco Community Center, the Greater Kansas City Community Foundation provided $75,000 in start-up capital for the International Dining Experience. The funds were not released, however, until Don Bosco's president had participated in the Denali Initiative, a social enterprise program headquartered in Pittsburgh, Pennsylvania. The curriculum, taught by university faculty, helps nonprofits hone the skills needed to launch a successful social enterprise, including development of business and financing plans.

WEIGH THE TAX IMPLICATIONS

If all the market research points to a feasible social enterprise, prepare a financial analysis that includes projected expenses, revenues, and break-even point. These projections, when considered as part of your organization's financial picture, and the nature of the venture itself (how closely related it is to your mission and purpose) will help you decide whether setting up a for-profit subsidiary may be the best route to take. (See Chapter 8 for more information.)

GOOD BUSINESS

Nonprofits have a long history of finding creative ways to fulfill their missions. Through social entrepreneurship they can leverage their existing strengths — such as dedicated volunteers, community support, and unique skills or services — through the application of for-profit business principles.

In other words, social entrepreneurship can offer the best of both worlds: meeting the challenges and demands of the marketplace while fulfilling the organizational mission.

If carefully conceived and thoughtfully implemented, a social enterprise can become self-sustaining. Then it can provide funds that give the organization freedom to undertake other programs and initiatives without always having to approach donors and grantmakers first.

Making Everything Pay Off

Case in Point: Pioneer Human Services

Seattle, Washington

Few, if any, nonprofits can match the entrepreneurial prowess exhibited by Pioneer Human Services. The majority of its $55 million annual budget comes not from fundraising or development efforts but from income earned through the sale of products and services. The competitive businesses operated by Pioneer provide many of its clients with employment and job training opportunities, furthering the nonprofit's mission to help people "realize personal, economic, and social development through participating in an integrated array of training, employment, housing, and rehabilitation services."

Founded in 1962 by an attorney who had been convicted of embezzlement, Pioneer offers a chance to change to alcoholics and other chemically dependent persons, convicts, work-release participants, and former offenders. In its first 40 years, Pioneer grew to employ approximately 1,000 people and serve more than 6,000 client customers annually. Much of that growth came through creating businesses to support services to clients, rather than contracting services out.

Social enterprises operated by Pioneer include

- numerous apartment buildings and a hotel, which provide lodging to low-income people and those in recovery from drug and alcohol abuse

- an in-patient chemical dependency facility

- six community corrections centers for ex-offenders making the transition back to society

- mental health and chemical dependency counseling services

- a construction company that not only works on Pioneer properties but also accepts third-party roofing and siding jobs

- three retail food locations, plus a unit that prepares and delivers more than 750,000 meals annually to Pioneer programs and third-party customers

- a distribution services business to handle assembly, packaging, and warehousing for customers that include toy companies

- two manufacturing plants that specialize in sheet metal fabrication and producing parts for airliners

Pioneer also assists other nonprofits, notably through its food buying service (which distributes food to more than 400 food banks and non-profit groups in 25 states) and its consulting service (which provides support in the areas of program outcomes measurement and entrepreneurial analysis and assistance).

All activities are undertaken with the idea that they will be self-supporting, provide environments for human growth, and generate the resources Pioneer needs to fulfill its mission.

SUGGESTED ACTION STEPS

1. Brainstorm at a board meeting the organization's current philosophy toward self-sufficiency and the potential implications (such as public perception) of engaging more visibly or deeply in social entrepreneurship.

2. Invite a qualified board member to volunteer to work with the chief executive to champion social entrepreneurship.

3. Before pursuing a social enterprise, require staff to develop a full-blown business plan for presentation to board members and potential funders.

8.

For-Profit Subsidiaries

One of our programs is making too much money, putting our nonprofit status in question. Should we consider forming a for-profit subsidiary?

Nonprofit organizations typically face this question when one of their activities unrelated to their tax-exempt purpose begins generating significant revenues. Such an unrelated, commercial activity can threaten the organization's tax-exempt status when it becomes substantial in comparison to exempt (related) activities.

Although the Internal Revenue Service (IRS) does not define substantial, a general rule of thumb is to consult with your legal counsel and accounting firm when unrelated business activities generate more than one-third of your organization's income.

UNRELATED BUSINESS INCOME TAX (UBIT)

Unrelated business activities that generate gross income of $1,000 or more annually are subject to unrelated business income tax (UBIT). The Internal Revenue Service requires nonprofit organizations to pay UBIT on net income derived from activity that is

- a trade or a business, intended to generate income by selling goods or performing a service

- regularly carried on, in a manner that mirrors the frequency and continuity of a similar activity conducted by a for-profit venture

- unrelated to the performance of the nonprofit organization's tax-exempt purpose

For example, nonprofit organizations typically pay UBIT on income from sales of advertising in their publications and on income from the sale of merchandise that is not substantially related to the organization's purpose. (Sales of educational books may not be subject to UBIT, while sales of T-shirts or coffee mugs might be.) Investment income — revenue generated by royalties, dividends, and interest — is *not* subject to UBIT.

If your organization is subject to UBIT, ensure that detailed business records are kept; the costs directly associated with the unrelated business activity can be deducted. If unrelated business activities account for gross income of $1,000 or more, even if those activities produce a net loss after costs are deducted, your organization will need to file Form 990-T with the IRS. (Unlike Form 990, this tax return does not have to be made public.)

GOOD REASONS TO PROCEED

In addition to maintaining their tax-exempt status or reducing the amount of UBIT incurred, nonprofit organizations may want to create a for-profit subsidiary to

- **Limit their legal liability.** With appropriate controls in place, the parent organization can be shielded from the legal risks associated with the business activity. Because legal and regulatory requirements

NONPROFIT SUBSIDIARIES

A spin-off organization can, like its parent, be a nonprofit organization as well. An organization may wish to create a separate 501(c)(3) entity to accept tax-deductible contributions for a specific educational or charitable purpose, such as awarding scholarships.

Typically, a parent organization and its nonprofit subsidiary have interlocking, or overlapping, boards. The parent retains control over who serves on the subsidiary's board, often drawing on its own board or executive committee members to do double duty. Alternatively, the parent organization can take the ex officio approach, naming certain individuals (such as the chief executive and board chair) as ex officio vary by state, be sure to consult your organization's legal counsel if this is a consideration.

- **Engage in a greater variety of activities.** The nonprofit's organizational documents or operating policies may restrict its ability to participate in the revenue-producing activities. These could then be undertaken by a stand-alone entity (either for-profit or nonprofit).

- **Better focus attention and resources.** By establishing a separate business, your organization is making a statement that it believes the activity is important. Whether the for-profit business involves publishing, insurance or employee benefits, financial services, group purchasing, or sales and marketing services, it will have its own staff, board of directors, and financial reporting requirements. This frees the parent organization to concentrate on other areas demanding attention.

- **Compete on a level playing field.** For-profit subsidiaries are better positioned to take on commercial competitors, which do not operate under strictures that may be imposed by a nonprofit organization. For instance, a magazine published by a subsidiary may be able to cover people or topics deemed too controversial by the parent organization; a subsidiary may be able to bring a product or service to the market much faster if it operates independently of the parent organization's formal budgeting and approval process.

---

members of the subsidiary board. Typically, the parent wants to control the majority of appointments to the board.

However similar their boards may be, the two organizations must maintain distinct operations. The parent organization's board may hold a meeting and then immediately reconvene as the subsidiary's board, but a separate agenda and separate minutes are required.

When boards overlap, it's advisable for the parent organization to further maintain control by requiring the subsidiary to request approval of any amendments to its governance documents (such as bylaws). The parent may also retain the right to remove any directors that it appointed to the subsidiary's board.

- Reduce the likelihood of mixed messages. A profitable business activity might raise eyebrows among those who believe a nonprofit organization should, at best, break even. Such an activity might also confuse potential members, community supporters, or donors who find the reality of the organization's operations differs from their perceptions; they may believe the nonprofit enjoys an unfair advantage in the marketplace because of its tax-exempt status and thus should not compete with local businesses.

Setting up a separate entity can reduce these concerns by keeping stake-holders focused on the parent organization's mission and minimizing any confusion about its true intent.

For-profit subsidiaries tend to be established as corporations, with the parent organization owning at least 51 percent of its subsidiary's stock. Other people can also hold stock or equity in the spin-off corporation.

KEEPING A DISTANCE

If, after consulting with legal counsel, your board believes a for-profit subsidiary will help generate revenue as well as provide valuable products or services, you'll need to take the steps necessary to spin off an activity. Bona fide intent should guide your decisions; in other words, you must make every effort to establish the subsidiary as an entity separate from the parent organization. Make sure to consider the issues described below.

WRITTEN AGREEMENTS

A parent organization may have every intention of giving its for-profit subsidiary full independence. But directors and circumstances change, so formalizing the type of relationship between the two organizations can provide continuity and help resolve any issues that arise.

In the agreement, spell out the operational arrangement (facilities supplied, rent paid, and so forth), in addition to accountability and communication procedures. If, for instance, the parent organization grants full editorial freedom to its publishing subsidiary, the parent should not become involved if a stakeholder becomes upset about something that appeared in a newsletter or magazine; the publishing subsidiary should handle the matter.

Like any partnership, the relationship between a parent organization and its subsidiary depends upon a high level of trust. Otherwise, each is likely to second-guess the other and create more problems than the subsidiary's establishment was intended to resolve. Maintaining this trust falls primarily to the chief executive officer of the parent organization.

INDEPENDENT BOARD, STAFF, AND RECORDS

The nonprofit may appoint the subsidiary's board of directors but by bringing in outsiders, the parent organization fosters independence between itself and the subsidiary.

Further, the subsidiary needs its own management team — some of whom may work for the parent organization as well. Staff members who work for both entities need to keep accurate records of their time and expenses. It's not unusual for a parent and its offspring organization to share employees and facilities, especially at the outset, but all those involved should record allocations of direct and overhead costs on a quarterly basis.

To be competitive in the marketplace, the subsidiary may have to offer higher salaries and incentive pay to attract staff with for-profit experience. Be aware that this can be a bone of contention, and a morale issue, for the nonprofit's staff.

The subsidiary should also convene its own board meetings, keep minutes of those meetings, and have its own bank accounts and financial reports.

HANDS-OFF MANAGEMENT

Even if a parent organization owns 100 percent of its subsidiary's stock or equity, it needs to take a hands-off approach to the subsidiary's day-to-day management and operations. A parent organization that exerts too much influence might lead the IRS to conclude the subsidiary is not truly a separate entity, and that could lead to a loss of tax-exempt status.

It's important to note that setting up a subsidiary does not exempt the parent organization from UBIT. If the parent organization owns more than 50 percent of the for-profit subsidiary's stock, any interest, rent, or royalties paid to the former by the latter may constitute unrelated business income and be subject to taxation. If the parent organization owns 100 percent of the subsidiary's stock, however, income could be paid in the form of dividends, which are not taxable. An attorney with expertise in the nonprofit sector can help you sort out the options.

STRATEGIES FOR SUCCESS

In 2001, before launching its for-profit subsidiary, the American Society for Microbiology (ASM), Washington, D.C., did extensive research on how other nonprofit entities had fared with their commercial ventures. Through interviews with consultants, lawyers, and staff of the subsidiaries, supplemented by in-depth reading, ASM identified characteristics common to for-profit ventures that had thrived and those that had faltered.

What ASM learned led to the creation of ASM Resources Inc., a for-profit subsidiary that researches and promotes commercial applications of scientific and technological advances in microbiology. The company aims to extend these advances to other fields such as medicine, public health, agriculture, and environmental sciences. ASM Resources was designed to embody the best practices of successful subsidiaries, which include

1. hiring employees with corporate experience relevant to the subsidiary's operations, not necessarily people from the nonprofit sector. That may mean recruiting and compensating people with expertise in retail, sales, financial services, or electronic commerce.

2. selecting a board of directors with experience in the subsidiary's area of operations and in the for-profit world

3. setting up the subsidiary as an autonomous organization, not as another business unit or department. Ideally, the subsidiary should have separate business facilities and reimburse the parent organization for services provided (such as accounting or administrative support) at fair market value.

4. ensuring the parent organization's board of directors, staff, and other stakeholders understand the objectives of the for-profit subsidiary

5. granting the subsidiary operational independence. Decisions should not require approval from the parent organization. (In fact, ASM discovered that involvement by the parent organization in the subsidiary's day-to-day decision making was the one factor common to subsidiaries that had failed.)

6. maintaining frequent contact between the parent organization and its subsidiary. The former should remain informed of the latter's setbacks as well as its successes.

7. approaching the creation of a subsidiary as any other business decision, with a market analysis, business plan, and financial projections

8. determining the parent organization's tolerance for financial risk: How patient can it afford to be? At what point will it require a return on investment?

9. providing adequate funding to establish the subsidiary, either by drawing on reserves, offering a line of credit, or soliciting contributions

10. keeping profit expectations low, especially during the subsidiary's first few years of operation

11. licensing the parent organization's trademarks or brands to the subsidiary to help it gain recognition and capitalize on existing relationships

12. encouraging the subsidiary to develop its own brands and trade marks as it becomes established as a separate entity

13. keeping the number of initiatives undertaken by the subsidiary to a handful. This focuses efforts and can help build market share.

14. ensuring the initiatives undertaken by the for-profit subsidiary advance the mission and values of the parent organization

Strength in Numbers

Case in Point: Medem, Inc.

San Francisco, California

By the late 1990s, consumers had become accustomed to researching medical conditions and treatments via the Internet, much to the dismay of many physicians who questioned the credibility of some of the information posted online. Seven professional societies, representing two out of three physicians in the United States, decided to do something about the situation. In October 1999, the seven organizations put up a total of $6 million in seed money to start an Internet corporation named Medem — short for medical empowerment.

Their goal was to create a patient-focused, Internet-based company to distribute health care information and enhance communication. Competition from commercial Web-based ventures already existed, but the seven groups saw their foray into the Internet as a natural extension of their missions to protect public health and strengthen the patient-physician relationship.

The various societies would provide and screen editorial content, ensuring the delivery of trustworthy, credible information to consumers. The corporation also hired a separate staff and set up independent operations. Within five months, Medem had attracted the attention of a private equity firm, which invested $20 million in the endeavor. The initiatives undertaken and trademarked by Medem include

- Medem.com (www.medem.com), a consumer-oriented Web site that includes access to the online medical libraries of more than 20 medical societies and a find-a-physician service that is searchable by geographic area, specialty, and name. The site is free to consumers.

- Your Practice Online, a service that enables individual physicians or group practices to develop a customized Web site. Patients visiting their doctor's site can easily link to the resources available on medem.com.

- Online Consultation, a service that allows physicians and their patients to communicate online through a secure connection. Medem has also developed guidelines governing such communication.

- Virtual Secure Network, which allows medical centers and hospitals to purchase Medem's services and tools to develop a local network that features secure online communications between them and physicians and patients.

The seven founding societies cover the spectrum of medical specialties, and include the American Academy of Ophthalmology (San Francisco, California), American Academy of Pediatrics (Elk Grove Village, Illinois), American College of Allergy, Asthma & Immunology (Arlington Heights, Illinois), American College of Obstetricians and Gynecologists (Washington, D.C.), American Medical Association (Chicago, Illinois), American Psychiatric Association (Washington, D.C.), and American Society of Plastic Surgeons (Arlington Heights, Illinois). Since Medem's founding, more than 40 other medical societies at the state and national levels have joined the electronic network as partners, giving their members access to Medem's offerings for physicians.

Medem's owners have not ruled out the possibility of offering stock to the public; according to the company's charter, only tobacco companies may be excluded from involvement. Five percent of the company is owned by the Medem Trust, a charity that earmarks its profits to provide health care services to the poor.

Suggested Action Steps

1. Ask an attorney and accountant to brief the board about the legal and financial advantages of establishing a for-profit or nonprofit subsidiary.

2. Determine your organization's tolerance for financial risk: How soon would a new subsidiary be expected to show a return on investment?

3. Appoint outsiders to serve on the board for any new subsidiary,

Part III

Strategic Alliances

9.

Cause-Related Marketing and Corporate Sponsorships

Staff have asked our board to develop policies related to cause-related marketing and corporate sponsorships. What's the difference between the two? And what makes them different from traditional corporate funding?

To attract charitable contributions and grants, successful nonprofits position themselves as partners with corporations, foundations, and other big donors. There's a win–win philosophy at work: The donor writes a check to the nonprofit and receives recognition, community goodwill, the satisfaction of advancing corporate objectives, and either a tax deduction or business expense; the nonprofit is able to advance its educational or charitable mission.

Often, however, corporations are one-time or occasional donors. They may support a high-profile capital campaign or a new initiative but not see the potential for a continual relationship. By developing a corporate sponsorship program or engaging in cause-related marketing, a nonprofit can take a corporate relationship to the next level, formalizing or structuring it as an ongoing partnership.

In the process, the emphasis typically shifts away from the corporation's grantmaking entity (corporate citizenship) to its marketing department (corporate promotion). In other words, you're no longer talking about philanthropy but rather a business deal.

FOR A GOOD CAUSE

Cause-related marketing refers to a situation whereby every time a customer makes a purchase, the company makes a contribution to the designated nonprofit organization. One of the original proponents of this approach is American Express. In fact, the financial services corporation is often credited with inventing the term.

In 1983, American Express raised $1.7 million for the foundation overseeing renovations of the Statue of Liberty and Ellis Island by donating one cent every time one of its charge cards was used. Cardholders responded enthusiastically, with use jumping 28 percent during the promotion. American Express profited not only through increased transaction fees but also from its connection to an American icon. The arrangement enhanced its corporate image as well as its bottom line, which is exactly the outcome that corporations seek from cause-related marketing.

Here are some other examples:

- Through its Take Charge of Education program, Target Corporation, Minneapolis, Minn., donates a percentage of annual purchases charged using its branded credit cards to the particular elementary or secondary school designated by each cardholder.

- In 1995, the Longaberger Company in Dresden, Ohio, launched its annual Horizon of Hope Campaign, held every July and August. The company donated $2 from each sale of a special handwoven basket to the American Cancer Society, generating approximately $1 million annually for breast cancer research and education. When its initial five-year commitment ended, the Longaberger Company renewed for another five years, describing the relationship as "a labor of love for all those involved, including millions of customers, independent sales associates, and our employees," many of whom are women. In addition to receiving the funds, the American Cancer Society distributes educational materials with each basket purchased.

- Ipswitch, a computer software company in Lexington, Massachusetts, designated several nonprofits as beneficiaries of its promotional efforts, including the American Heart Association, American Red Cross, and Child Welfare League of America. Each time customers purchased a particular product, they could select the nonprofit of their choice to receive a royalty. (The company also developed an internal program, enabling every employee who had a baby to designate one of several nonprofits to receive a $500 corporate contribution.)

Signing Up Sponsors

Corporate sponsorships are nothing new. Just think of how long businesses have been buying uniforms for local Little League teams. In the 1990s, however, such business arrangements became more widespread. Eat a particular cereal, and you support the U.S. Olympic Team. Drink a specific brand of coffee, and you help save the rainforest. Purchase a certain piece of clothing, and you can aid a children's welfare organization. In fact, several research studies have confirmed that consumers are more likely to purchase products from companies that exhibit active community involvement. In addition, employees whose companies team up with nonprofits usually feel a greater loyalty to their employers.

Corporate sponsorships typically involve a specific product or signature event, although sometimes they apply to an organization's activities in general. One group, which publishes the definitive handbook in its field, recruited a sponsor for every chapter so the cost of producing an updated version was kept to a minimum. Each sponsor's name was also tied to educational seminars based on the book's various chapters. And sponsorships don't necessarily have to be in the form of a cash donation. A regional group has developed a partnership with an airline, which provides a specific number of round-trip tickets each year. That enables the nonprofit to attract big-name speakers to its events without paying travel expenses and to offer promotional prizes to attendees.

Some organizations have found the piecemeal approach to sponsorships can be wearing on them and corporations alike. It's increasingly common for nonprofits to develop corporate partnership programs with specified levels of involvement. That is, as a company invests more with the organization, it moves up the sponsorship ladder and in return receives more benefits, such as recognition and public acknowledgments. By making an upfront commitment, a company can enter its fiscal year without worrying about when the organization will come knocking at its door for assistance, and the organization can plan its programs accordingly.

The Internal Revenue Service (IRS) keeps close watch on sponsorships, which, unlike advertising, are not subject to unrelated business income tax (UBIT). Therefore recognition of sponsorships is allowed, provided it does not constitute advertising. Based on the final regulations, published by the IRS on April 25, 2002, you can thank corporate sponsors by listing their Web site addresses and other contact information, providing neutral descriptions of their products and services, and publicly announcing their name.

WORKING IT OUT

No matter what type of relationship you'd like to establish with a company, take time to do the following:

- Determine what you have to offer. Evaluate your organization realistically: Can you offer demographics that companies might desire? Do you organize a well-known event? Can you provide an entree into a market niche that would otherwise be difficult for companies to access? Even with marketing personnel on staff, you might want to hire an outside agency or consultant to help craft the value proposition and seek out sponsors.

- Figure out what drives the company. What is behind the company's desire to establish a formal relationship with your organization? What is its motivation? Although being a good corporate citizen is laudable, there's usually more to the story.

- Research your partner. Check out the company's Web site, annual reports, and media coverage. Find out what you can about its financial stability, status in the field, and corporate citizenship initiatives. What kinds of complaints have been filed against it? What kudos has the company received? Consider convening a focus group of stakeholders to hear the word on the street and get their impressions of potential partners. You want to know as much as possible about any company to which you plan to link your name, logo, and reputation.

- Make a good match. What you're looking for is a close fit between your organization's objectives and your partner's business objectives. The arrangement should add value from the perspective of both parties by complementing mission, identity, and values. That consistency translates into success in the marketplace: The general public is more likely to participate in a program that makes sense to them.

- Acknowledge the give and take of a true partnership. Certainly, you'll want to develop policies to guide creation of corporate relationships. Just don't make them so restrictive that you don't have room to negotiate. For instance, rather than requiring the company to put in all money upfront, you might develop a royalty formula based on performance criteria. That shows your willingness to work together, not just accept a charitable contribution.

- Be willing to walk away. As a board member with an eye on financial health, it's difficult to say "no thanks" to the potential for additional revenues. But if the company and your organization don't have compatible cultures and goals, managing the partnership may not be worth the organization's precious resources. It may take so much staff time that other priorities, such as conducting mission-oriented programs or an annual fund drive, suffer as a result.

POLICY DEVELOPMENT

The larger your organization's scope and reach, the more likely you'll be approached by corporations eager to establish some type of ongoing relationship. That's not to say that local corporations aren't interested in pursuing such partnerships as well, but your organization may need to take the lead. What works for multinational corporations and global nonprofits can also work for local agencies and businesses.

ADDITIONAL OPTIONS

Nonprofits have a variety of options for generating revenue, including

- **Affinity programs.** Whether offered by credit card, car rental, or overnight shipping companies, these programs pay royalties to the nonprofits in return for use of their names, logos, and mailing lists. If someone carries a credit card with your organization's logo, for instance, you'll receive a royalty every time the card is used. These programs differ from sponsorships because they already exist; the nonprofit simply signs on as one of the participants. In contrast, corporate sponsorships are custom-crafted to meet the unique needs of the two parties.

- **Revenue-sharing programs.** Found often on the Internet, these pro-grams involve a merchant or retailer of goods and services paying a royalty or commission to the Web site's owner based on leads, refer-rals, or actual sales. For instance, Amazon.com has agreements with numerous nonprofits: Visitors to a nonprofit's Web site can click on a link to purchase books from the company, and Amazon.com pays a royalty based on the amount of the sale.

Although staff — or a marketing agency you have contracted with — will contact potential partners and handle the ensuing negotiations, the board has a role in policy development. Assuming all board members are comfortable with the idea of corporate partnerships, draft guidelines that discuss

- **Appropriate partners.** Ensure that you are not linking your organization's good name and reputation with a company that might undermine its mission. For instance, a health-related organization probably wouldn't want to partner with a company that manufactured or distributed tobacco or alcohol products. The connections are not always obvious, especially with multinational corporations, so research on potential partners should not be undertaken lightly.

- **Minimum guidelines.** Some organizations require a three- or five-year commitment from their corporate partners; anything less rarely provides enough time for building brand equity for either the sponsor or the nonprofit. Others ask for a guaranteed level of financial support before they will consider forming a relationship.

- **Licensing agreements.** Through licensing, you give a company the right to use the organization's intellectual property (such as a trademarked or copyrighted name, logo, or slogan) in exchange for royalties. Licensing agreements are often part of revenue-sharing and affinity programs, but they can stand on their own as well. When Christian Dior introduced a new perfume named Dune, it compensated the Nature Conservancy for use of the organization's logo, which appeared on informational materials on dune ecosystems. Another group licensed its name and logo to an automobile manufacturer, which promoted the group in all of its print and electronic advertising. The nonprofit achieved what it couldn't afford on its own: national brand identity.

- **Publishing royalties.** Several high-profile writers have earmarked the proceeds from sales of certain books to benefit a nonprofit. As an example, Barbara Kingsolver, a best-selling author, selected Heifer International in Little Rock, Arkansas, as one of the organizations that receives royalties from a book of essays she produced. Kingsolver, noting she has "a special interest in food production, along with the abiding hope for cultural respect and global justice," selected Heifer International because it gives gifts of livestock to impoverished families.

- **Uses of your organization's name.** Insist on having final approval on advertising copy and images, media vehicles selected, promotional wording, and so forth. If you don't maintain this control, you risk having your organization marketed in a manner that may be at odds with its values and mission. For instance, legal experts recommend that nonprofits avoid using the word endorsement in any promotional material; the organization could be found liable if something was wrong with product or service it endorsed. Note, however, that all marketing activity itself must be handled by your corporate partner, unless you're willing to pay UBIT. If your organization becomes actively involved in promotion, it may violate IRS regulations that require a passive approach to tax-exempt income.

- **List restrictions.** To keep stakeholders from becoming annoyed, determine how often (if ever) you will provide your mailing list to corporate partners. This may be determined by privacy guidelines you already have in place, such as not releasing the e-mail addresses of visitors to your Web site.

- **Staff liaison.** Hold the chief executive accountable to oversee all cause-related marketing and sponsorship efforts. Duties should include approving contracts and promotional language, tracking royalty payments, and ensuring both parties fulfill their contractual obligations.

- **Recognition guidelines.** How will you say "thanks" to your partners? Although the staff liaison should have some freedom to negotiate with individual corporations, board policy should dictate where to draw the line. For example, your policy may require board approval for a ttaching a sponsor's name to a signature event. But the board doesn't need to get involved in operational details, such as how often the sponsor will be acknowledged in an organizational publication or how big its logo will appear on the Web site.

- **Exclusivity.** Will your organization maintain an exclusive relationship with the company for length of the contract, not pursuing relationships with similar companies? Most, if not all, companies will insist on exclusivity.

- **Written contract.** Describe every detail of the business arrangement, including which party provides what and when. If a company provides you with its standard contract, don't hesitate to negotiate changes on points you may be uncomfortable with. In fact, you may want to develop a model contract of your own, in consultation with your organization's attorney. Also ask legal counsel to review any contract in advance, with a special emphasis on structuring the arrangement to minimize tax consequences.

SCORING BIG WITH SPONSORS

CASE IN POINT: US YOUTH SOCCER

Richardson, Texas

Each year US Youth Soccer registers approximately 3.2 million players between the ages of five and nineteen, split evenly between boys and girls. With such coveted demographics, it's no wonder that corporations are interested in aligning themselves with the nonprofit group. In fact, US Youth Soccer fields at least 10 calls a week from companies seeking to get their names in front of young soccer players, as well as their parents and coaches.

Only those committed to enhancing the US Youth Soccer brand make the cut. Thirteen corporations have signed sponsorship agreements, which range from three to 20 years, and provide the organization with multimillion-dollar revenues each year. As a result, US Youth Soccer has an official vehicle (Chevrolet), an official supplier (Adidas), an official hotel (Holiday Inn), an official bottled water (Aquafina) and soft drink (Pepsi), and even an official laundry detergent (Tide). Each agreement is exclusive and contains elements tailored to the individual company.

At its headquarters, US Youth Soccer dedicates three full-time employees to marketing. In addition, it employs four regional marketing coordinators; their responsibility is to ensure that the state associations in their respective regions comply with the terms of the national sponsorships. To sell the sponsorships, the organization relies primarily on the expertise of a sports marketing agency, which can also provide sponsors with creative, promotional, and public relations assistance.

Snickers is the official snack of US Youth Soccer and the name sponsor of its national championships. It has maintained its sponsorship relationship since 1993, when the company signed a 20-year agreement. The brand equity is evident: Research conducted by US Youth Soccer indicates that, in the world of youth soccer, Snickers is known almost as well as the organization's own brand.

Suggested Action Steps

1. Review success stories of cause-related marketing and corporate sponsorships during a board meeting; in breakout sessions, ask them to identify what your organization has to offer potential partners and what possible barriers might be encountered.

2. Develop board policies to guide staff on such issues as selecting appropriate partners, using the organization's name and logo, and providing recognition.

10.
Partnering with Grantmakers

We have an opportunity to undertake an exciting project, but we can't do it alone. How can we attract significant support from a committed partner?

Even if your organization has ventured successfully into social entrepreneurship and signed up corporate sponsors, you still probably depend upon the generosity of donors to accomplish many of your goals. Launching a high-profile program or new initiative can help you get a foot in the door with donors who may have been on your prospect list for some time. It forces you to investigate other funding sources that may turn out to be quite receptive to your grant proposal.

IDENTIFYING GRANT SOURCES

Grants are typically available from a variety of organizations. Each type of organization has its own proposal or application requirements and criteria for distributing their awards; the competition among grant-seeking entities varies as well. Several sources are described below.

GOVERNMENT

Agencies from the federal level on down to the state, county, and local levels draw on taxpayer dollars to effect change in communities. Some federal funds are distributed through the states, based on a formula for disbursement, and require you to file applications at the state level. Locally, you may find grants are available through such entities as a school district, a parks and recreation board, and a county health department.

PRIVATE FOUNDATIONS

Established to carry out a specific mission, private foundations are required by the Internal Revenue Service (IRS) to disburse a certain percentage of their funds each year. Depending on how their portfolios have performed in a given year, private foundations may (or may not) be seeking proposals from many different organizations.

COMMUNITY FOUNDATIONS

The focus of community foundations is usually the community, not a specific mission. They may award grants within a very wide range of projects and they may also manage donor-advised funds.

CORPORATIONS

Many companies have made a commitment to being good corporate citizens. This includes visibly supporting activities that assist the communities in which they do business and that reflect positively on their corporate image. Larger corporations tend to have a designated department or even a separate foundation to handle grant requests.

INDIVIDUALS

People who fall into the category of major donors may be willing to provide a grant for a specific project that promises to provide them with psychological, social, or emotional satisfaction. Motivations may include honoring a family member, making a public statement about personal beliefs, or giving back something to a supportive community.

Increasingly, foundations as well as individuals are adopting a philosophy of venture philanthropy. In some ways a return to the era of philanthropists such as Andrew Carnegie or John Rockefeller, who often took high-profile and active roles on behalf of a cause, this philosophy emphasizes personal involvement of the donor. It's more than writing a check to a nonprofit. Venture philanthropists want to make a more personal connection by:

- **Becoming visibly engaged in the organization's activities.** This may range from serving on the board to taking a hands-on approach and interacting directly with clients or stakeholders.

- **Influencing how the charitable contribution is actually used, to ensure every dollar counts.** Those who have been successful in business often want to put their budgeting, investing, and management skills to use in the nonprofit sector as well.

- **Wanting the charities of their choice to produce quantifiable results, just as for-profit businesses do.** Many favor funding projects that reflect an entrepreneurial mindset or rely on free-market competition.

MAKING A GOOD MATCH

It's crucial to view your organization's relationship with any type of grant-maker as a partnership: You're in this together. Your organization devotes its energies and resources to a project, and the grantmaker helps make it all financially possible. The grantmaker is able to fulfill its own mission while helping your organization fulfill its purpose, with publicity often in the mix as well. Any grant proposal your organization submits should spell out the benefits for both parties, which in turn translate into helping the people at whom the project is targeted.

DUE DILIGENCE

Just as a potential funder evaluates your organization, you need to figure out whether the partnership would be of reciprocal benefit. Although it's tempting to go after as many funds as possible, take the time to be selective. Developing a detailed proposal may be a wasted effort if, for example, the funder sets criteria that you can't meet at the moment.

Evaluate potential partners in terms of

- **Amount of average grant.** If you're seeking $15,000 in support, you may want to hold off on calling funders that typically write checks for $150,0000. They probably don't want to devote administrative time to your small-scale proposal. Conversely, if the funder typically awards $5,000 to grantseekers, you'll need to contact additional prospects to cover your anticipated costs.

- **Requirements to match funds.** Some grants come with the caveat that the nonprofit organization demonstrate community support of its initiative by raising matching funds within a specified amount of time. The grant is rescinded if the effort to obtain matching funds falls short. In some instances, grantmakers will accept volunteer hours (calculated at a specific hourly rate) to fulfill part of the matching requirement.

Whether a grantmaker disburses public or private funds, it will have the same primary goal: funding projects that mesh well with its own objectives. In your written proposal and in person, you must be able to articulate your organization's value proposition — how your initiative will advance or support the values held by the donor.

This isn't always easy, especially if the grantmaker has a broad mission. You'll need to research the type of grants awarded in the past, to detect any patterns and identify what elements of your organization's programs or services may resonate with the donor. Grantmakers often post their funding guidelines on their Web sites; you can also review their annual reports for valuable clues.

- **Conditions.** Some foundations take a venture-capitalist approach to grantmaking, seeking ongoing influence in the way their money is spent on a start-up project. They may ask to place a representative on your organization's board of directors or a high-profile committee, a request that may not mesh with your current culture or policies.

- **Eligibility.** To be eligible for a grant, you may be asked to team up with another organization proposing a similar project, to avoid duplication of efforts. Again, this requirement may put undue stress on your organization, especially if the other group is charged with taking the lead on the project and has a vastly different approach in mind.

- **Reporting requirements.** Most grantmakers will ask you to measure outcomes in a certain way. Make sure that complying with their conditions will not strain your human and financial resources, or consider building those additional costs into your proposal.

- **Future funding requests.** You might encounter a grantmaker that funds only start-up initiatives or won't renew grants to ongoing programs after a few years. Make sure you'll have other means to continue the work you start.

Also assess the competition for the grantmaker's dollars. How many proposals does it typically receive each year? How many grants are awarded? Be realistic about your chances for success.

Your strongest prospects are the funders who support projects and organizations with characteristics much like your own. Look for a good match in terms of target audience, geography (local versus regional versus national), delivery (how and when), content (the topic or issue you are addressing), and cost (how much, when, and for how long).

As an example, here are excerpts from the guidelines for grantseekers issued by the Ewing Marion Kauffman Foundation in Kansas City, Missouri:

> The Kauffman Foundation only funds programs within the United States. The majority of our Youth Development grants go to organizations within the Kansas City metropolitan area. . . . In general, Kauffman Foundation grants are limited to programs and/or initiatives that have significant potential to demonstrate innovative service delivery, community support, and/or public policy opportunities in support of youth and entrepreneurs. . . . We do not fund capital campaigns, construction projects, endowments, special events, or international programs. . . . Grant size ranges from a few thousand to several million dollars, depending on the size of the organization and the scope of the project.

If an organization believes one of its projects is a good match, the Kauffman Foundation suggests submitting a letter of inquiry, preferably fewer than three pages in length. Other grantmakers will have their own distinct requirements, processes, and procedures, so be prepared to tailor your proposals accordingly.

WHAT FUNDERS SEEK

Every grantmaker is unique and will look for different types of opportunities and organizations to fund. Don't hesitate to ask what a particular grantmaker may want from your organization, in terms of information, preparation, involvement, or recognition. You might not even ask for direct monetary support. Some grantmakers will consider in-kind contributions. One supporter, for example, has its in-house print shop produce many of the materials distributed by a local nonprofit, with no cost to the group. Another company routinely donates raw materials to nonprofits constructing or renovating their buildings.

Beyond seeking a good match with their values, your potential partners will also evaluate what your organization has to offer in such areas as those described below (the list is by no means inclusive).

COMPOSITION OF BOARD AND STAFF

The Bill and Melinda Gates Foundation, for one, pays attention to the type of board members and the quality of staff in every organization it considers funding: What have they accomplished thus far? Another organization looks for volunteer leaders who exhibit entrepreneurial knowledge and skills. Still another favors funding organizations whose boards clearly reflect their mission and principles, such as having geographic, ethnic, and socioeconomic diversity. Having staff dedicated to development is a plus, as is low turnover in those positions, which enables your organization to build consistency and strengthen relationships over time.

BOARD INVOLVEMENT

Even with dedicated staff in place, grantmakers like to see board members taking ownership of development activities. This should not come as a surprise to new board members. When you recruit, provide potential board members with a list of expectations, including making personal contributions, soliciting contributions from others, and identifying potential funding prospects (public and private).

BOARD AND STAFF FUNDRAISING SUPPORT

It's not enough for board members to solicit others; they need to reach into their own pockets as well. After all, funders may argue, if the organization's leaders don't believe in a program enough to support it, why should they? Some grantmakers may be interested in the amount of the average board gift, but most look for the percentage of participation (ideally, 100 percent).

Grantmakers may also look at employee participation and commitment as an influencing factor. Do employees believe in what the organization stands for? The level of participation, not the size of the gift, is what matters.

A STRONG TRACK RECORD

What your organization has been able to accomplish in the past can greatly influence whether you receive the funds to launch a future initiative. How effective has the organization been at achieving its goals in the last two, five, or even ten years? Even a relatively young organization must be able to present evidence of how it is making a difference. Face it, people like to back a winner.

Statistics That Relate to the Grantmaker's Own Mission

The way you track and report data probably doesn't mesh exactly with the type of programs supported by a particular grantmaker. Be prepared to consolidate or repackage your budget and service delivery information and to recast it in the language used by a potential funder. Taking those steps makes it easier for decision makers at the grantmaker to compare various proposals and weigh the benefits of each one.

Anecdotal Evidence of Benefits

Personal stories, told either in person or on paper, can be powerful counterpoints to pages of statistics. If privacy laws permit, ask for testimonies from clients, customers, or other recipients of your efforts. If possible, bring one of them to a grant-proposal presentation to put a human face on your organization's mission.

Creativity

Find a way to catch the attention of grantmakers, who review hundreds, if not thousands, of requests each year. Are you proposing something different, perhaps a new way to approach an age-old problem?

Organizational Efficiency

Grantmakers often want to know what percentage of each dollar raised your organization devotes to programs, compared to administrative costs. Industry watchdogs have suggested that nonprofits spend 45 to 50 percent of their total incomes on programs and activities directly related to their missions. Also, look at other organizations in your area that work with similar issues and use them as a benchmark to measure of your own efficiency at allocating resources. Talk to your auditor to find out the average in your area. Your board could also establish target figures that reflect your organizational culture; use that percentage as a measure of your own efficiency at allocating resources.

Organizational Transparency

The BBB Wise Giving Alliance also requires nonprofits to provide, upon request, annual reports and annual financial statements that include significant categories of revenues and expenses (such as fundraising costs). Share these documents with grantmakers, along with information on how the board makes decisions and allocates resources.

Ongoing Communication

In addition to making the Form 990 readily available to the public, some watchdog organizations suggest that nonprofits provide, upon request, annual reports and financial statements to those who desire additional financial data. Be forthcoming and share these documents with grantmakers — even before receiving a request.

Donors' Rights, Your Responsibilities

In 1993, the Association of Fundraising Professionals (then the National Society of Fund Raising Executives) joined with the American Association of Fund Raising Counsel, the Association for Healthcare Philanthropy, and the Council for Advancement and Support of Education to promulgate guidelines for receiving charitable gifts. The resulting document, known as the Donor Bill of Rights, offers a helpful checklist for any nonprofit organization intent on fulfilling its responsibilities to grantmakers. It reads as follows:

> Philanthropy is based on voluntary action for the common good. It is a tradition of giving and sharing that is primary to the quality of life. To ensure that philanthropy merits the respect and trust of the general public, and that donors and prospective donors can have full confidence in the nonprofit organizations and causes they are asked to support, we declare that all donors have these rights:

I. To be informed of the organization's mission, of the way the organization intends to use donated resources, and of its capacity to use donations effectively for their intended purposes.

II. To be informed of the identity of those serving on the organization's governing board, and to expect the board to exercise prudent judgment in its stewardship responsibilities.

III. To have access to the organization's most recent financial statements.

IV. To be assured that their gifts will be used for the purposes for which they were given.

V. To receive appropriate acknowledgment and recognition.

VI. To be assured that information about their donation is handled with respect and with confidentiality to the extent provided by law.

VII. To expect that all relationships with individuals representing organizations of interest to the donor will be professional in nature.

VIII. To be informed whether those seeking donations are volunteers, employees of the organization, or hired solicitors.

IX. To have the opportunity for their names to be deleted from mailing lists that an organization may intend to share.

X. To feel free to ask questions when making a donation and to receive prompt, truthful, and forthright answers.

The organizations have drafted a complementary E-Donor Bill of Rights that outlines the best practices for soliciting funds online. The guiding principles include these expectations of online donors:

- To be assured that all online transactions and contributions occur through a safe, private, and secure system that protects the donor's personal information.

- To be clearly informed if a contribution goes directly to the intended charity, or is held by or transferred through a third party.

- To not receive unsolicited communications or solicitations unless the donor has opted in to receive such materials.

Copyright 2002, Association of Fundraising Professionals (AFP), formerly NSFRE, all rights reserved. Reprinted with permission.

Suggested Action Steps

1. Invite the development director or a fundraising consultant to speak to the board about the various types of grantmakers and the criteria typically used to evaluate proposals.

2. Ask staff to develop a process for evaluating potential funders, to ensure the time invested in preparing proposals is directed toward the top prospects.

3. Encourage board members to participate in presentations to grantmakers, bringing their unique perspective to the table.

11.
Mergers and Acquisitions

Our mission and service delivery area overlap with those of another organization. It makes sense to team up, but how do we know if a merger or acquisition is right for us?

As merger mania swept through corporate America in the 1990s, it was only natural that the trend should extend to the nonprofit sector. Seeing their memberships shrink as two, three, or even four companies became one, some trade associations followed suit and merged themselves simply so they could survive. The American Automobile Manufacturers Association was so hard hit by international mergers in that industry that it simply closed its doors in 1998.

For groups seeking grants and charitable contributions, mergers affected the funds available as well. Instead of having two companies writing checks for $5,000 each year, a social service agency might receive one check — for $5,000, not $10,000 — after the two companies merged and reviewed their community contributions. If the merger involved a multinational corporation with headquarters elsewhere in the country or abroad, the prospect of local financial support dimmed further.

But it's not just groups facing an economic downturn that look into a merger. Heightened competition throughout the nonprofit sector — for top-notch staff, attractive benefits, political clout, media recognition, you name it — has prompted healthy, wealthy groups to seek partners with whom they can achieve even greater success.

In 1995, for example, the National Coal Association merged with the American Mining Congress. Although both organizations had been in existence more than 75 years, one primarily represented coal mining companies in the east and the other mainly represented hardrock mining in the west. The two joined forces with one goal: to serve as the united voice of America's mining industries and present their views to legislators, journalists, and the general public. The prevailing philosophy was to incorporate the best of both organizations into a new one: the National Mining Association, Washington, D.C.

Technically speaking, a merger involves two partners that agree to integrate their processes, programs, governance, and staff; a new name is often selected to reflect the fresh start being made by both groups. An acquisition refers to one organization gaining control of another and folding the latter into its own structure. One professional society, for instance, acquired a smaller society that served a niche market within its scope of membership. The acquiring group maintained the other society's name and membership benefits but integrated it into existing operations, viewing it internally as one of several membership councils rather than a separate entity. At first, little changed for members of the acquired group except that their dues decreased. Then they realized that many more networking opportunities, publications, educational seminars, and conferences were available to them, all at the lower cost. The economies of scale had kicked in, providing one of the most attractive elements of a merger or acquisition.

Before even mentioning the word *merger* in the same breath as another organization's name, consider collaborating in some way, if time permits. Two groups, for instance, might form a purchasing group, jointly hire a legislative monitor, or even coordinate an event or program together. Each group maintains its autonomy and makes no commitment to working together again. This option provides an opportunity to learn about the other organization's culture and gauge the willingness of both boards to explore a more formal strategic alliance.

Then you might look into sharing administrative services, sharing office space, or launching several joint programs. Both groups remain independent but begin to share the decision-making process and some systems. The next step could be a merger, which involves restructuring both organizations and integrating all functions.

KEY CONSIDERATIONS

If as a board member you have felt the urge to merge, answering these questions can help you clarify your organization's unique situation.

WHY ARE YOU CONSIDERING A MERGER?

Zero in on your goals. Do you seek organizational growth, a greater diversity of services, a wider geographic scope, a larger market, an enhanced public profile? All of those are valid reasons for a merger, as are realizing greater economies of scale and achieving a greater concentration on core competencies (doing more of what you do best). And if you are contemplating a merger because your organization may collapse financially without one, state that as well. This self-assessment should also include an honest appraisal of your organization's strengths and weaknesses, what makes it an attractive merger partner, and what the potential drawbacks are.

Poll all the board members, and you might be surprised by the range of responses. Only after leaders reach unity on organizational goals and agree on the results they expect from a merger can they approach another group at the negotiating table.

One caveat, mergers cost money. You'll need to pay attorneys, accountants, organizational consultants, printers, and information technology experts, to name just a few. You may need to craft an attractive severance package for your chief executive. Plus, there are the hidden costs, such as the time devoted by staff to working out details, handling rumors, or simply being too distracted to do their jobs effectively. So if the motivating factor is short-term economic survival, broaden your perspective. A merger is for the long term.

HOW COMPATIBLE ARE YOUR MISSIONS?

Chances are, you are already aware of your potential partner's history, reputation, programs, and financial situation. Still, you'll need to conduct due diligence and thoroughly investigate the other group. Be sure to pay attention to the other organization's mission. Is it similar to your own? Complementary? Even if the groups employ very different strategies, are they, at heart, focused on the same ends? Mergers can be challenging enough on their own; you need a mission on which both can agree to serve as the island in what may be a turbulent sea at times.

WHAT DO STAKEHOLDERS THINK?

Conduct surveys and focus groups with staff, community members, business leaders, funders, clients, customers, members, and so forth. Ask for their opinions on your organization's current situation, including its strengths and weaknesses. Identify concerns they may have about the organization potentially losing its identity through a merger or, conversely, what possibilities might open up if your group joined forces with another.

During the research phase, some groups find that, to the wider community, they are virtually indistinguishable from their competitors anyway so a merger would simply clear up existing confusion. Others discover emotions run so deep that a merger would alienate key stakeholders. You won't know unless you ask.

WHAT ARE THE CULTURES OF THE TWO ORGANIZATIONS?

As objectively as possible, assess the values that guide the way each organization currently does business. Determine what your organization values and rewards (for instance, flexibility, risk taking, personal development, or cross-departmental initiatives). What is your perception of the other group? How manageable might the differences be?

Certainly, each organization will have its own procedures and traditions where board and staff are concerned. Assuming the bedrock beliefs that drive each group are similar, such as the mission, then any feelings of us versus them should subside, when given enough time and effort by all parties. Organizational experts say the best way to create a new culture is through communicating honestly and handling conflict (instead of avoiding it). Ideally, what emerges is a new culture entirely, one with its own traditions.

WHO CAN HELP GUIDE THE PROCESS?

An outside perspective is invaluable, especially when emotions run high in the boardroom and among staff who don't know what's happening behind those closed doors. After all, a merger might mean a chief executive, other employees, and some board members won't have roles within the new organization.

Hire an attorney or a consultant who has an expertise in nonprofit mergers. He or she will ask questions and raise important issues that might otherwise be ignored and can assist with developing an implementation timetable should the merger occur.

CONVERSATION STARTERS

Here's a quick checklist of the types of issues both organizations will need to agree on before a merger of the two can become a reality. All may have far-reaching implications, financially, operationally, or emotionally. It's best to have a merger negotiations committee with equal representation from both groups (including the chief executives) work through these issues. In addition, an outside consultant or facilitator will help keep the discussions on track.

GOVERNANCE

- Mission of the merged organization
- Vision for the future
- Name of the new organization
- Size and composition of the board of directors
- Board leadership and succession
- Number and type of committees

STAFFING

- Selection of chief executive
- New staff structure
- Compensation, benefits, and severance policies (if positions will be eliminated)
- Personnel policies (vacations, performance evaluations, workweek, dress code, and so forth)

FINANCES

- Selection of information system
- Selection of accounting system

- Current assets and liabilities
- Pending lawsuits
- Estimated costs of merger
- Commitments from funders and donors (especially those with restrictions)
- Fundraising calendars

PROPERTY

- Location of headquarters
- Sale or purchase of space
- Additional properties owned or leased
- Maintenance requirements

PROGRAMS

- Number, type, and range of programs offered
- Consolidations
- Delivery areas and modes
- Training
- Evaluation and outcomes measurements

MARKETING AND COMMUNICATIONS

- Name, logo, slogan
- Plan for informing employees
- Plan for informing the public, including funders
- Communication plan if merger does not go forward

When Two Become One

Case in Point: The Family Tree

Baltimore, Maryland

The Family Tree grew out of the 1997 merger of Parents Anonymous of Maryland and the Child Abuse Prevention Center (CAPC). The impetus came from the chief executives of the two organizations, both of which were successful, volunteer-driven agencies that offered programming to prevent child abuse and neglect.

Because of their similar missions, the two groups often found themselves competing for the same grant money. Both were also similar in size: One had 15 staff and an annual budget of $950,000; the other had 11 employees and a $700,000 budget. At the same time, the organizations had complementary characteristics. Both operated satellite offices but in different counties. One had a strong infrastructure, while the other's strength was in programming.

At the suggestion of their chief executives, the boards of both groups began contemplating the financial, programming, staffing, and governance implications of a merger. Research indicated that forming one organization would increase the range and accessibility of services for parents and families and would provide one voice for public policy development and advocacy on the issue of child abuse prevention.

Eight months after the initial merger proposal, Parents Anonymous of Maryland and CAPC became one organization. Their experiences offer food for thought for any group with merger on the mind.

To guide the merger, the groups formed a committee with equal representation from each board (the board chair and two additional members). The committee decided that the first board chair of the merged organization would be from Parents Anonymous, with CAPC providing the board chair the next year, and that the new board of directors would incorporate both former boards, minus those members who chose to relinquish their roles.

Both chief executives expressed interest in leading the new organization. When the merger committee announced its intention to settle the issue by conducting a search for a new leader, the chief executives compromised. One became executive director of the new group, the other deputy executive director. Interestingly, within 16 months of the merger, the executive director and several senior staff resigned; the board selected a new chief executive who had no previous affiliation with either group.

The merger committee spent a lot of time on financial projections and, through foundation grants, raised $150,000 specifically to cover merger expenses. These funds paid for moving offices, producing new letterhead and promotional materials, and purchasing a new telephone system, among other expenses.

Shortly after the merger, the new organization was selected as the recipient of $200,000 in pro bono work provided by Eisner & Associates, a local advertising agency. The agency and the merged group solicited community input and came up with The Family Tree name, logo, brand, and advertising strategy. The agency also recommended keeping the names of the two former organizations, in small print, on all public relations materials for the first three years.

Although unified under a new name, staff and board members had to grapple with differences in the two organizations' cultures. One customarily worked a 35-hour week, the other a 40-hour week, and vacation and performance evaluation policies differed. When staff were combined, pay differentials emerged. In some cases, managers were making less than their direct reports.

For the first two years, The Family Tree's staff was split between two buildings (administrative in one, programming in another). This hindered integration and upgrading of internal systems and infrastructures. It then purchased a new headquarters to better consolidate operations and realize economies of scale.

Thanks to careful budgeting and continual fundraising, The Family Tree operated in the black from its inception. The new organization successfully enhanced its image in the community through public relations and marketing, expanded the geographic reach of its services, introduced several new programs, and developed a results-based system of accountability and evaluation to assess its effectiveness in meeting organizational objectives.

In hindsight, however, board and staff identified two elements that might have made the whole merger process less stressful yet just as successful. They would have spent more time on due diligence during the negotiations phase and would have hired an attorney or consultant to guide the merger process and raise potential issues or concerns from the start.

Source: Philadelphia Health Management Corporation, Nonprofit Strategic Alliances Project (www.phmc.org).

Suggested Action Steps

1. Invite board chairs from similar types of organizations in your area to meet informally to discuss potential areas of collaboration or coordinated activities.

2. If a merger is a strong possibility for your organization, appoint a board-level task force to conduct due diligence on the other group and develop recommendations for a smooth blending of the two staffs, cultures, and operational structures.

3. Consider hiring a consultant to facilitate merger discussions and help bring the two groups together with minimal problems.

Part IV

In the Public Eye

12.
Risk
Management

Last year our organization became involved in a lawsuit that unexpectedly damaged our reputation and drained our resources. How can we guard against this happening again?

When a legal issue arises, it's not just the nonprofit organization but also its elected leaders who potentially have a lot to lose. The legal aspects of serving on a nonprofit board may surprise some directors who see the position as an honorary one or as recognition of community or professional achievements. In fact, board officers and directors may be named in lawsuits filed against the organization. Ignorance of illegal activity is not an adequate defense.

In one state, a nonprofit board was held liable for the organization's failure to pay payroll taxes. In another instance, an employee claimed the board had her fired after she reported internal wrongdoing. Bottom line: The board remains accountable for the organization's actions.

AREAS WORTH WATCHING

Having clear policies and enforcing them is the best form of protection. A board can reduce its risk by establishing and periodically reviewing policies and procedures related to the six key areas described below.

EMPLOYMENT

Legal experts report that the majority of lawsuits filed against nonprofit organizations pertain to personnel issues. These cases run the gamut from discriminatory hiring to wrongful termination, from sexual harassment to breach of contract. Recommended practices include the following:

- Ensure anyone in a position to hire or terminate employees understands and complies with state and federal laws. These usually relate to employment interviews and procedures for termination.

- Develop position descriptions that clearly spell out the job-related qualifications and performance criteria.

- Conduct thorough reference and criminal background checks on all employees.

- Follow a formal process for conducting annual performance reviews, including a written plan agreed to by the employee and manager, for improving skills or competencies.

- Provide a means for employees to report fraudulent, discriminatory, or harassing behavior without fear of reprisal. For example, an employee who believes she is being harassed by the chief executive should be able to freely report the situation to someone else in the organization.

- Establish a process for handling potential disputes, such as calling in a third-party investigator, a mediator, or an arbitrator. Taking steps toward alternative dispute resolution may lead to a compromise and keep the issue out of the legal system.

- Have legal counsel regularly review employment applications and personnel handbooks to ensure they comply with recent developments in employment law.

GOVERNANCE

In most states, the laws require nonprofits to maintain certain corporate records, such as meeting minutes and rosters of voting members, and make them available upon request. Minutes should reflect whether a quorum was present; legal challenges are possible if a decision was not made by a majority vote.

Various documents related to tax-exempt status, in addition to employment records, must either be maintained or filed annually, all of which points to the need for record-retention policies. Ensure that board members are familiar with applicable federal and state laws and receive notification when the organization fulfills its reporting requirements (such as making the three most recent Forms 990 available to the public upon request on your organization's Web site).

Be sure to brief board members on the potential for conflicts of interest (see Chapter 13). Ask board members to annually disclose any potential conflicts of interest so their fellow directors can take that information into account when making decisions.

FINANCIAL ACTIVITY

A board may choose to delegate some duties to a finance committee, such as budget development and quarterly reporting, but it remains accountable for the organization's financial health. The board's best defense against a claim is being able to show, through meeting minutes and other documentation, that it exerted appropriate oversight.

With the assistance of an external auditor, ensure that appropriate internal controls exist to record transactions, approve or authorize expenditures (especially above a certain level), safeguard assets, and comply with state and federal reporting requirements. Set guidelines for the reimbursement of travel expenses and the use of a corporate credit card or charge account. Also have a policy detailing how any financial discrepancies will be investigated (see Chapter 16).

KEEPING THEM COVERED

Here are some suggestions for obtaining insurance coverage to protect volunteers from liability:

- Select an agent or broker who not only works with nonprofits but also specializes in directors and officers (D&O) insurance (sometimes referred to as association professional liability or APL insurance).

- Negotiate. Rarely does a standard policy match an organization's specific requirements. Explain the organization's needs, based on the activities it undertakes and sponsors.

- Clarify what the policy will cover: Attorney's fees? Fines? Penalties? Punitive damages? In most states, D&O insurance does not cover civil fines, such as those assessed by the Internal Revenue Service (IRS). Also find out whether the insurance company will reimburse your organization for the costs incurred or pay them directly.

BUSINESS OPERATIONS

To minimize risk, organizations should develop written contracts for big-ticket items or services purchased from suppliers or contractors. True, a contract can exist between two parties without being put in writing but you're more likely to remember all the tasks and details involved when obligated to record them.

Ensure contracts include standard language and provisions, such as appropriate use of trademarks, terms of payment, a cancellation clause, and a mechanism for dispute resolution. Ask your attorney to review any contracts that involve large expenditures, and don't hesitate to propose changes to contracts supplied by vendors.

FUNDRAISING

It's helpful to have policies that outline what type of gifts and grants the organization will accept and the extent of due diligence required before a decision is made. Receiving federal grant money, for instance, generally requires a nonprofit to provide reports that may prove cumbersome for a

- Pay attention to the exclusions, which might include claims of libel, slander, antitrust violations, and sexual harassment. Also, some policies exclude employees or directors who receive compensation. Consider paying additional premiums (or engage in negotiations) to cover the excluded areas.

- Decide on which policy limits and deductibles are most appropriate for your organization.

- Find out whether the policy covers past acts or only those claims that occur and are reported during the time the policy is in force. You might want to extend the coverage into the past.

- Always notify the insurance company of any actual or anticipated lawsuit or claim. If you fail to give notice of a claim — to the company, not just the agent — within a specified period of time, coverage may be denied.

small staff to produce; if those reports are incomplete or aren't filed on a timely basis the grant could be in jeopardy.

Will you accept restricted gifts (to be spent only as specified by the donor) or gifts of buildings or land? One organization, offered an aging office building as a gift, discovered that it could not afford to make the modifications needed for the building to conform to the Americans with Disabilities Act (ADA). Another one turned down a gift of property when an environmental analysis, required by board policy, turned up evidence of a garbage dump decades earlier. Had the organization accepted the property and later discovered that the ground water was contaminated by hazardous waste, it would have been responsible for an expensive clean-up effort.

VOLUNTEERS

Double-check that your general liability insurance covers injuries that volunteers, employees, or other visitors may sustain while attending an event sponsored by the organization or held at its facilities. Also, to reduce the likelihood of discrimination claims, have standardized procedures in place for recruiting and terminating volunteers.

FOR ALL TO SEE

The Internal Revenue Service (IRS) may assess tax penalties on nonprofits that fail to file Form 990 (Return of Organization Exempt from Income Tax). This annual report of revenue, expenses, assets, liabilities, and income-producing activities is due five months after the close of the organization's fiscal year, on the 15th of that month.

Typically, the staff prepare Form 990, often with the auditor's assistance. It is the board's responsibility, however, to ensure that this happens. Otherwise, the organization may have to pay a penalty based on every day the tax return is late.

The IRS may also assess penalties on an organization that does not make its three most recent filings of Form 990 available for public inspection.

PROVIDING PROTECTION

Numerous protections — some minimal and some substantial — exist for board members. If a nonprofit is incorporated, for instance, state laws may limit the personal liability for officers and directors who are unpaid volunteers and who do not engage in willful or reckless conduct.

In 1997, Congress enacted the Federal Volunteer Protection Act to encourage volunteerism by limiting liability. The act protects unpaid volunteers acting within the scope of their organizational responsibilities at the time, provided their actions do not lead to criminal misconduct or gross negligence. It does not prevent volunteers from being named in lawsuits, nor does it protect them from civil rights violations (such as discrimination) and sexual harassment offenses. The Volunteer Protection Act does not protect the organization itself; it can still be held liable for the actions of its volunteers.

To further shelter volunteers from personal liability arising from legal actions, nonprofit organizations indemnify board members, usually through a resolution or bylaws provision. Based on the state's laws, indemnification may allow the organization to reimburse a volunteer for legal expenses incurred or to pay the cost of any damages assessed, unless fraud, gross negligence, or criminal activity occurred. Should litigation and expenses total thousands or even millions of dollars, the organization must shoulder a significant financial burden and may have to drain its reserves.

By law, an organization must comply immediately with any in-person request to review its Form 990 during normal business hours. Alternatively, an organization has 30 days in which to comply with a written request (letter, fax, or e-mail) and may charge a reasonable fee to cover copying and postage costs. According to the IRS (www.irs.gov), an organization does not have to fulfill individual requests if it makes its tax returns widely available, such as posting the forms on its own Web site or on an online database of nonprofits such as GuideStar (www.guidestar.org). The names and addresses of contributors to the organization (unless it is a private foundation) are withheld from public disclosure.

In addition, most states require nonprofit organizations — especially those that engage in fundraising — to file annual financial reports, along with a list of officers, directors, and trustees.

Of course, indemnification is meaningless if the organization doesn't have sufficient funds or assets to cover the costs of legal actions against its volunteers. That's why most organizations purchase directors and officers (D&O) liability insurance. This coverage is in addition to the organization's comprehensive general liability (CGL) policy, which covers claims related to property damage, theft, and bodily injury. In contrast, D&O insurance protects against harm resulting from decisions made by the board, including employment practices, mismanagement of finances, and antitrust violations. Many policies will also pay the legal fees related to the coverage areas, even if the lawsuit is considered frivolous or the allegations prove to be without merit.

When the chief executive and board of directors abide by a code of conduct and work together to develop comprehensive policies and procedures, the organization has a good chance of limiting potential liability for all parties. Purchasing D&O insurance coverage provides the organization with added protection and gives key volunteers peace of mind as they fulfill their fiduciary and governance responsibilities.

PERSONAL LIABILITY CHECKLIST

Just to be on the safe side, board members should do the following to minimize the risks of board service:

- Do your homework before voting on an issue. Thoroughly review background materials, especially any legal or financial documents.

- Take time to deliberate before casting a vote. Ask thoughtful questions, and don't allow yourself to be rushed into a decision.

- Ensure that the meeting minutes reflect any dissenting votes.

- Review the monthly and quarterly financial reports, and read the auditor's annual report.

- Disclose any potential conflicts of interest.

- Always act in the best interest of the organization.

NOT ABOVE THE LAW

CASE IN POINT: ENRON CORPORATION

Houston, Texas

Although Enron is a for-profit company in the energy industry, the actions of its board of directors hold valuable lessons for corporate and nonprofit boards alike. Because of questionable accounting practices by Enron's outside auditor and financial improprieties internally, its board members came under fire for allegedly breaching their fiduciary responsibilities.

As a result of the company's collapse in 2001, thousands of employees lost their jobs and investors lost billions of dollars. The chief executive and other high-ranking officials resigned amid charges of deception and fraud. The federal government launched an investigation to determine the extent of wrongdoing.

Although the situation is still unfolding, the news media has reported that Enron's board

- voted to suspend the company's code of conduct, including the avoidance of conflicts of interest. This enabled Enron officials to participate in outside partnerships.

- did not act prudently in how it administered the company's Employee Stock Ownership Plan related to its 401(k) retirement plan. That included not providing employees with sufficient information about the true value of Enron stock.

- approved financial reports and balance sheets that did not report all debt

The board has taken the position that top Enron managers and outside auditors withheld important information and did not follow board-approved procedures. One might argue that the board deferred too much to management and the auditing firm and didn't raise the questions that might have uncovered financial irregularities. In any case, employees who saw their life savings and jobs disappear filed numerous lawsuits against the company.

Board members may be found liable if the employees prove intentional misconduct occurred; D&O insurance would not cover that offense. The insurance carrier may also deny coverage if it can prove that the board knowingly disguised the company's financial position when the policy was written.

Suggested Action Steps

1. Conduct a risk management and legal audit to ensure your board and staff have policies in all applicable areas.

2. Review with board members the scope of the Volunteer Protection Act and your organization's indemnification policies.

3. Periodically review your organization's insurance policy pertaining to directors' and officers' actions.

13.
Conflicts
of Interest

We often recruit board members because of their prominent position and influence within the community, their ties to a particular company, or their extensive network of contacts. How can we ensure that a real or perceived conflict of interest doesn't occur?

The professional expertise and personal contacts a board member brings to a nonprofit organization can be invaluable. Ethical violations or other improprieties are hardly, if ever, on the minds of those who agree to serve an organization that is dedicated to doing charitable, educational, or humanitarian work.

It is actually their desire to serve the organization that may prompt board members or employees to engage in activities that, to outsiders, have conflict of interest written all over them. These activities may involve — but aren't limited to — financial dealings. Wanting the organization to save some of its precious dollars, a board member may offer his or her legal expertise to draft contracts or agreements. The board chair may capitalize on the position's high profile and be named to the board of a funding agency to keep an eye out for the organization.
An employee may suggest channeling business to a start-up firm, which happens to be owned by a family member.

Whatever the situation, lapses in ethical or moral behavior can instantly attract media attention and draw the ire of the community: The public's trust is violated when people appear to profit from a nonprofit's activities.

Note: Information presented in this chapter is not intended as a substitute for legal advice. For the latest details on legal developments, including state and federal laws regarding nonprofit organizations, consult an attorney with expertise in those areas.

Recommended Practices

Conflicts of interest, sometimes referred to as duality of interest, happen all the time. In fact, they're inevitable, but they are also manageable. Just because a board member has two separate and competing interests at heart doesn't mean a crisis is in store for the organization. What you want to avoid is any appearance of impropriety, which can be as damaging as an actual occurrence of it. An awareness of what potentially constitutes a conflict of interest and subtle reminders of board members' obligations can keep everyone focused on what's best for the organization.

The board chair should work to cultivate an atmosphere in which board members feel comfortable discussing their personal and professional interests and asking about those of their colleagues. A collegial board is more likely to identify and ask about potential conflicts of interest in a nonthreatening manner.

Work with legal counsel to develop a disclosure statement that would identify potential conflicts of interest. Present the statement for each board member's signature annually, perhaps in conjunction with the board's self-assessment, board retreat, or annual planning meeting.

Assure board members that the statements will remain confidential and be disclosed only to an attorney or auditor should a serious problem arise. The statement, in a nonthreatening manner, should ask the board member to

- disclose personal or professional affiliations (including those of immediate family members) with companies the nonprofit organization does business with. Board members should report, for instance, whether they hold a sizable amount of stock or have other financial interests in a company.

- disclose any personal business dealings (including those of immediate family members) he or she has had with the nonprofit organization in the previous 12 months

- list other corporate or nonprofit boards on which he or she (or an immediate family member) serves. This will reveal whether a board member may be put in the position of deciding whether or not the nonprofit organization receives funding from a corporation, foundation, or agency.

When recruiting new board members, identify conflicts of interest that may arise and explain the disclosure policy they will be asked to sign. If a major conflict of interest seems likely to arise during his or her term in office, you may want to postpone that person's election to the board.

Develop guidelines for identifying and handling potential conflicts of interest:

- Before voting on an agenda item related to an expenditure or the awarding of a contract, the board chair should ask all directors whether a potential conflict of interest exists.

- When a conflict of interest has been identified, the board member should excuse himself or herself from the discussion and the decision. The board chair may need to issue a reminder, perhaps mentioning the disclosure form.

- If a conflict of interest comes to the attention of the organization, designate who will discuss it with the board member involved (for example, the board chair or the executive committee). Include a provision for addressing conflicts of interest that involve the board chair.

Playing It Safe

To avoid putting itself in a situation where intermediate sanctions are likely, your organization should follow these steps:

1. Develop a conflict-of-interest policy that requires full disclosure. In addition to reviewing the policy with board members, educate them on the IRS penalties associated with financial transactions that provide excess benefits to organizational insiders.

2. Require full board approval on annual budgets and financial audits.

3. In advance, submit large transactions to the board for review, consideration, and approval. The discussion should uncover any potential conflicts of interest and, based on data gathered in advance, touch on whether the transaction is at fair market value and accurately reflects what comparable organizations would pay for the same products or services. Such data are available from lawyers, CPAs, and other independent experts.

4. Keep good records of decisions made by the board, including dates and terms of transactions. Meeting minutes should include the names of any board members who abstained from voting on particular transactions because of a potential conflict of interest.

- Removal from the board should be the last resort. If managed well, conflicts of interest do not escalate into clashes of personalities or tests of wills.

Realizing that a conflict of interest exists does not mean the nonprofit organization can't do business with a particular company or has to pass up a fund development opportunity. It simply means the board of directors must be aware of, understand, and scrutinize the situation from all angles before proceeding with a decision.

Ultimately, an organization must trust its judgment in selecting board members on whom it can depend to do the right thing: Be loyal to the organization and promote its best interests rather than their own personal agendas.

5. Maintain separate financial records and follow separate decision-making procedures for sister organizations. If your organization, for instance, is a (501)(c)(3) and operates a for-profit subsidiary, the parent should receive the most benefit from the relationship. Compensating the subsidiary for performing a service may be considered an excess-benefit transaction if the amount paid by the parent is far above the marketplace average for a comparable service.

6. Consult with legal counsel and develop a checklist to guide financial decision making. These guidelines will ensure your organization is taking the appropriate action to avoid excess-benefit transactions and can help provide a safe harbor from intermediate sanctions. For example, one area likely to attract attention from the IRS is executive compensation (including health benefits, retirement benefits, incentive plans, and other perquisites). When determining the chief executive officer's salary and benefits, the board should research compensation packages offered to comparable nonprofit and for-profit organizations; link the executive's compensation to personal and organizational performance; and keep records indicating when the full board or one of its committees makes a formal decision on the executive's salary.

7. Stay up to date on developments in this area, usually available on the IRS Web site (www.irs.gov).

On the Staff Side

The potential for a conflict of interest is not restricted to the board of directors. The actions of staff can also raise eyebrows within the community — and attract undesirable media attention — when they appear to be at odds with the organization's image as advancing the public good.

Recommended practices related to employees include the following:

- Establish procedures for obtaining competitive bids on outsourced jobs. For instance, require that every job costing $1,000 or more be put out for bid to at least three vendors. This step shows that employees have conducted cost-comparison research and provides supporting documentation if the contract is ultimately awarded to someone having ties to the organization.

- Ask staff to update conflict-of-interest forms annually. These forms should be similar to those signed by the board of directors.

- Prohibit staff members from serving on the board of directors, which sets policies and makes financial decisions that affect their livelihood. One exception: the chief executive. Many organizations designate the chief executive as an ex officio (nonvoting) member of the board.

- Develop a policy that prohibits staff from devoting time on the job or using office equipment to pursue projects for personal gain, whether financial or professional. If an employee writes a book, operates a business, or runs for public office, for instance, he or she must do it outside the workplace to avoid any appearance of impropriety.

Intermediate Sanctions

Laws governing conflicts of interest within nonprofit organizations vary from state to state. In some states, laws provide for the removal of board members or the appointment of new management should there be proof of personal gain as a result of service to a nonprofit.

In addition, the federal government in 2002 issued its final regulatory requirements, primarily in response to high-profile cases involving questionable financial activities undertaken by tax-exempt organizations. These regulations underscore that serving as a trustee, officer, or board member of a nonprofit organization can have significant personal tax liabilities and should therefore be viewed as a serious responsibility.

They apply to 501(c)(3) organizations — excluding private foundations — and (501)(c)(4) organizations. Organizations classified under Section 501(c)(6) of the Tax Code are not affected, although the private inurement doctrine still applies to them.

The requirements enable the Internal Revenue Service (IRS) to penalize individuals who take advantage of their positions inside nonprofits, rather than penalizing the entire organization by revoking its tax-exempt status. Known as intermediate sanctions, these regulations are spelled out in the Internal Revenue Code (Section 4958) and govern excess benefit transactions between a nonprofit organization and disqualified persons.

"Excess benefit" simply refers to any transaction that exceeds fair market value for the benefit received by the nonprofit or is not comparable to what similar organizations or companies pay for a similar product or service. Any financial transaction is subject to scrutiny, from severance payments to transfers of property to officers' liability premiums.

According to the IRS, the term "disqualified person" refers to anyone in a position to exercise substantial influence over the affairs of the non-profit organization within the preceding five years. This category would include officers, directors, trustees, high-level employees (including department managers), major donors to the organization, and even the families of all these types of people.

Should the IRS determine that a disqualified person has received an excess benefit, the person has a tax liability of 25 percent of the excess amount. (If the tax is not paid or the excess amount not returned to the organization within a specified amount of time, the penalty increases to 200 percent.) In addition, any board member or manager who knew of or approved the transaction is subject to a 10-percent tax on the excess amount (up to a maximum of $10,000 per excess-benefit transaction).

The IRS may waive the taxes and penalties should the nonprofit organization uncover the excess-benefit transaction and correct it before an IRS audit takes place.

SUNSHINE LAWS

Some states also have sunshine laws on their books. Alternatively known as open meeting laws, these regulations are intended to shed light on the inner workings of an organization and promote accountability by those in decision-making positions.

In general, the laws pertain to state governments and nonprofits that receive public funds (such as school boards). Some states have extended sunshine laws to cover nonprofits that have government contracts or have government officials serving on their board (which may be a condition of the funding).

Those affected by sunshine laws usually must meet certain requirements for notifying the public about meetings, making meeting locations accessible, and providing minutes of the meetings within a reasonable time. The laws do not prohibit closed meetings when certain confidential issues are under discussion, such as salaries, lawsuits, disciplinary actions, and personnel matters.

Even if your organization is not subject to sunshine laws, making efforts to operate in an open, accountable manner can increase public confidence in and support of your mission. That means intentionally providing the interested public with information on which it can evaluate your organization's performance, whether it's posting your Form 990 on your Web site or issuing an open invitation for people to attend board meetings.

The public often seeks such openness, or transparency, in regard to financial decisions. Your organization's stakeholders may also desire to know more about internal processes: How are leaders chosen? How are decisions made? How are plans and objectives established? Making non-confidential information readily available — even if someone is not specifically asking for it — can reduce any suspicions that may arise among staff, donors, the media, and even other board members. By being forthcoming with information, you prove yourself worthy of the public's trust.

Personal Opinion or Policy Statement?

Case in Point: Great Lakes Aquarium

Duluth, Minnesota

For years, an environmentalist had written a column for a local newspaper. When the Great Lakes Aquarium hired the columnist as its education director, there was the potential for his published comments to be construed as being representative of the nonprofit aquarium rather than his views as a private citizen. Voluntarily, the columnist removed his job title from his byline in the newspaper column.

In September 2000, the columnist expressed his views on a proposed power line. Specifically, he stated that installation of the power line would have a negative effect on the environment. The columnist did not mention the power company by name.

As it so happened, the power company in question had contributed more than $1 million to the Great Lakes Aquarium and its president and chief executive officer served on the aquarium's board. The company took the position that the columnist was well known in the community as the aquarium's education director and asked that its name be removed from any educational projects.

The aquarium's executive director shared the power company's response with the education director who, after several conversations, resigned his position. The local media had a field day with what transpired, printing the power company's letter (with its permission) and the reaction of the columnist (who emphasized that the aquarium was not part of the dispute). There was more to come:

- Two members of the aquarium's board resigned, protesting the departure of the education director.

- A citizens' group formed, demanding that the power company executive resign from the board.

- Duluth's mayor, who also served on the board, called for the citizens' group to disband so the aquarium's reputation wouldn't be hurt.

- A state legislator called for reinstatement of the aquarium's education director and the resignation of its chief executive.

- Staff members sent a letter to the board, protesting its treatment of the education director and questioning its effectiveness in upholding the aquarium's credibility.

If the Great Lake Aquarium had a crisis communications plan in place, it did not activate it. Rather, the board remained silent, which the public interpreted as support for the power company and its executive. In an editorial, the *Duluth News Tribune* took the aquarium to task for its handling of the issue. The newspaper noted: "If the precedent stands without word from the board, any individual board member or donor who disagrees with private views of employees on issues unrelated to the aquarium will be able to hold the aquarium hostage. Members of nonprofit boards in our community have a responsibility to safeguard their institutions from the whim of individuals."

SUGGESTED ACTION STEPS

1. Establish board guidelines for identifying and handling potential conflicts of interest; communicate these to incoming board members.

2. Develop a disclosure policy for each board and senior staff member to review and sign annually.

3. Look for ways in which your organization and its board can operate in a more transparent manner, such as posting nonconfidential information on a Web site and issuing open invitations to at least some board meetings.

14.
Crisis
Communications

The media just ran a story on our organization that has public relations disaster written all over it. What should we do?

Isn't it ironic that your organization works hard to attract media coverage — then, when you least want the attention, reporters are all too eager to delve into the details of a disaster, scandal, accident, arrest, demonstration, or other crisis?

Anything related to your organization's external or internal affairs can become the target of media scrutiny, from actions of board members and staff to incidents within the field or profession. Even if those incidents occurred elsewhere, reporters may contact your organization looking for a local angle. How you respond can negate years of good public relations work, or better position your organization for favorable coverage in the future.

PREPARE A PLAN

When the unthinkable does occur, a crisis management plan provides an excellent starting point for a response. A typical crisis management plan outlines who responds on behalf of the organization and how communications with various audiences are handled. Here is how to craft a crisis management plan.

BEGIN BY BRAINSTORMING

Gather staff members and key volunteers and ask them to identify everything that could go wrong for the organization — natural disasters, terrorist attacks, financial debacles, personnel conflicts, and so forth. Reviewing what has happened to other nonprofit groups is a good way to get this discussion started. Group the potential crises by broad category, such as economic, technical, and operational.

For each potential crisis, identify any preventive measures you should implement and those already in place. For instance, how often are computer files backed up and where are those files kept in case of fire? What accounting procedures do you have in place to reduce the likelihood of fraud or embezzlement? If communicated and enforced, such measures will reduce the number of crises likely to occur.

Next, ask the group to pare the list to the five most critical issues and develop a what if scenario for each. What if a tragedy occurred at an event? What if a large sum of money was discovered to be missing? What if a prominent board member publicly disagreed with the organization's well-known position on an issue? Talking through how the organization should respond in each instance will set the stage for developing the crisis management plan.

MEETING THE PRESS

Even the most savvy communicator can benefit from coaching provided by a media consultant. Participating in mock interviews will better prepare an organization's official spokesperson to appear comfortable, cooperative, and sincere in his or her dealings with the media.

The advice offered by media experts includes

- Say *something.* Uttering the phrase "No comment" is guaranteed to raise eyebrows among the public; like it or not, people will think you have something to hide. If you can't comment on a question asked by a reporter, explain why. Perhaps you don't have the information on hand or a law enforcement official has asked you not to release certain details.

- Speak to the public. Rather than answering the reporter's questions, think in terms of answering the public's inquiries. What would you like the general public to know? What words, phrases, or analogies would resonate with them? Focus on how people are affected by the information you have to offer.

SELECT THE CRISIS TEAM MEMBERS

Take a tip from the federal government, which appoints an incident commander for each emergency or disaster and then, depending on the scope of the crisis, appoints section chiefs related to such areas as planning, logistics, and operations. Having a command hierarchy in place when disaster strikes will reduce chaos because everyone knows where she or he should focus individual efforts.

Spell out who performs which tasks. You might, for instance, designate the chief executive as the incident commander and the public relations director as the media liaison and chief spokesperson. In some organizations the chairman of the board serves as the spokesperson; if that's your board's policy, be sure the person receives media training before taking office. Another option is to designate several spokespeople, each qualified to speak about a different aspect of the crisis but all working under the direction of the person in charge of the crisis response.

List contact information for every member of the team, including work, home, pager, cell phone, and fax numbers, plus e-mail addresses.

- **Don't fear silence.** Rather than rushing to answer a question immediately, take a few moments to gather your thoughts. Your pause won't appear in the newspaper and will be edited out of the evening news broadcast. If a question catches you by surprise and you need more time to think, use a filler phrase such as, "That's an excellent question. Here's what I think is important. . . ."

- **Take your time.** Speak slowly so you can better control your response and be able to emphasize key points.

- **Watch your body language.** Standing up straight communicates confidence and control; direct eye contact and holding your hands open conveys honesty and openness. On the other hand, sure signs of secretiveness include squinting, touching your nose, and covering your mouth.

- **Be brief.** When communicating your key messages, think in bullet points: The average television sound bite is 10 to 15 seconds.

Include a chart detailing the flow of communication — who calls whom — and designate a command center or meeting place for the team. Because a crisis can occur at any time, each member of the team should keep an updated copy of the roster at home, at work, and in his or her wallet.

IDENTIFY KEY AUDIENCES

Develop checklists of others to contact, such as local officials; regulatory agencies; civic, social, or other organizations that could also be affected; members of the business community; and media contacts. The latter may be unnecessary if journalists have already jumped on the story. If your organization has built credibility with members of the press, however, you might be able to provide additional information and shape the coverage to show your organization in a more favorable light.

Remember to include internal audiences, such as employees, board members, clients, major vendors, and significant donors. During tense times, it's tempting to focus on calming the media storm, but leaving internal groups out of the communications loop can have serious repercussions. A reporter may call a board member directly, putting that person on the spot and leading to a truthful, if undesirable, quote on the order of, "Nobody has told me anything."

Employees, especially those who answer the phones, need to be briefed, ideally in person so their questions can be addressed. In a pinch, e-mails, conference calls, or voice mails will work, too. Emphasize that employees as well as organizational volunteers should forward all media requests to the designated spokesperson rather than providing personal opinions.

Keep e-mail addresses and phone numbers updated as contact people change within the key audiences.

PREPARE BACKGROUND MATERIAL

Develop a fact sheet with bulleted points about your organization and its related field, industry, or profession. These can be distributed to media contacts as background while you are creating a fact sheet specific to the crisis at hand.

Have Board-Approved Policies in Place

The best time to address crisis management policies is when all is calm, when board members can objectively focus on ideal practices. The policies should address such questions as the following:

- Who is allowed to speak on behalf of the organization?

- What information is considered public, and therefore available for release to the media, and what is considered private? Your attorney can address what information might raise legal liability concerns.

- Who has the responsibility of calling a press conference? One organization, for instance, sanctions only those press conferences organized by the chief spokesperson; it also has a policy that all press conferences be videotaped.

- What is the organization's responsibility should serious injury or death result? Your policy may include paying for funeral expenses and expressing public condolences, when appropriate.

- How often should the crisis management plan be reviewed and revised?

Practice

Just as schoolchildren have regular fire drills, your organization should see how well it can respond to a fictitious crisis. You may be surprised at how rattled members of your team can become when a microphone, even a fake one, is thrust in front of them. Conversely, a drill can be just the assurance people need that they are well-prepared to do their assigned jobs in the midst of an emergency.

For authenticity, consider working with a media relations consultant to conduct the drill. This person can also provide feedback and insights to take into account before finalizing a comprehensive crisis management plan.

When a Crisis Occurs

Even with a plan in place, your organization can't possibly be prepared for every potential crisis. If you have prepared a plan and rehearsed, however, your response to an emergency situation is more likely to be calm and collected rather than driven by adrenaline. Make sure to follow the tactics outlined below.

RESPOND QUICKLY

Daily deadlines drive print and broadcast journalists; if the story is big enough, they will cover it without your organization's assistance. To ensure your perspective is acknowledged, have your spokesperson make contact with the media by calling a press conference (for complicated situations) or issuing a public statement.

The statement should present the basic facts of the situation as known at the time, provided that release of those facts — such as someone's name — does not raise privacy or liability concerns. Disseminating information quickly can help move a story off the front page. If reporters keep prodding your organization for more information, publicly state that you are committed to assembling all the facts and will release additional details as they are confirmed.

CRAFT YOUR MESSAGES

In addition to the basic facts (who, what, where, when) decide on the two or three main points you want to communicate. State your message, support it with facts and examples, and repeat the message, using the simplest language possible.

Of course, reporters will make every attempt to extract additional information through their questions. Acknowledge your desire to assist them, but don't take the bait and speculate on what might have happened or what could have been done differently. As a crisis unfolds, speculative comments can come back and harm your organization's reputation.

Before meeting with the media, have the crisis management team list the questions that reporters are likely to ask, probably in the bluntest of terms. Be prepared for questions such as, "Who is to blame?" "How was this situation allowed to happen?" "Is this due to bad management?" "Where was the board when all of this was going on?" Rehearse the responses until they sound polite, calm, and rational, not defensive or adversarial.

BE TRUTHFUL

If you don't have the answer on hand, or if you are unable to release information because of legal constraints, say so. Explain when you will be able to provide the information, or refer reporters to an appropriate source, such as the physician providing treatment if the crisis involved serious injury. If the organization has made an error, admit it.

Reporters are resourceful and often unwilling to let go of a story if they sense there is more to it: The truth will always come out. Your willingness to communicate honestly and straightforwardly with both external and internal audiences will help sustain the organization's good reputation.

ASK FOR HELP

Rely on friends and supporters, including other nonprofit organizations, to help you through a crisis. For instance, if a fire or natural disaster has destroyed your office, borrow space to temporarily set up shop. Turn to community providers for counseling services should your staff experience a tragic event.

EVALUATE YOUR ACTIONS

It's natural to want to put a crisis behind you as soon as possible. But don't be too hasty; many lessons can be learned from how your organization and the crisis management team responded.

After the dust has settled, assemble the crisis management team to review what went right and wrong. The team should prepare a written analysis that includes what happened, who responded first (and how), who notified various audiences, what media coverage resulted, and so forth. Any errors identified through the evaluation process can be used to improve the crisis management plan and the training provided to team members.

As unwelcome and as devastating as a crisis can be, your organization can use one to its advantage. By handling a situation calmly, effectively, and expediently, your organization can enhance its standing within the community and reinforce its mission and values.

HONESTY IS THE BEST POLICY

CASE IN POINT: UNITED WAY SILICON VALLEY

San Jose, California

The spring of 1999 brought a wake-up call to board members of United Way Silicon Valley, known then as United Way of Santa Clara County (UWSCC). First, they learned from local newspapers that the staff had been cut in half, with some employees walking away with attractive severance packages. Yet they also learned that the chief executive had depleted the organization's reserves; not only was the group coming up $11 million short in its fundraising campaign but also it would be unable to make the payments it had already promised to 100 agencies.

UWSCC's board immediately fired the chief executive. The board chair, Michael E. Fox Sr., stepped in to oversee daily operations and to face intense scrutiny from both the media and the community. He told the unvarnished truth: The board had missed all the warning signs pointing to financial disaster and had taken the chief executive's word for everything rather than asking probing questions about staffing, contributions, and expenses. Fox devoted at least four hours each day to speaking with reporters and opened UWSCC's books to anyone interested in reviewing them.

Fox's candor, including his own admission of error for not fulfilling his responsibility as board chair, fostered respect among reporters and community leaders alike. In addition to hiring a new chief executive, the board appointed an oversight committee to restructure UWSCC. Then, all the board members resigned, including Fox. These actions underscored the organization's desire to come clean and begin rebuilding its battered reputation.

In 2000, with a new board in place, UWSCC changed its name to United Way Silicon Valley (UWSV) to better reflect the area it serves. The organization's public acknowledgment of its mistakes and the steps it openly took to improve operations made an impression on donors as well. Several foundations and individual philanthropists made contributions totaling $14.6 million, which enabled UWSV to meet its funding commitments and get back on its feet financially.

Suggested Action Steps

1. Ensure your chief executive has an updated crisis management plan in place; it should be able to accommodate a range of situations, from a natural disaster to negative media coverage.

2. Periodically conduct drills with staff using a fabricated yet realistic crisis. This tests how well board and staff members are prepared to fulfill their roles as outlined in the crisis management plan.

3. Provide the board chair or other designated spokesperson with media training that includes mock interviews and press conferences.

Part V

Board–Staff Partnerships

15.
The Chief Executive–Board Chair Partnership

As the board chair, I'm well aware of the importance of a strong partnership with the chief executive. But recently we have been at odds on various issues, and I'm concerned we've reached a stalemate. How can I make my term in office more productive?

Like a marriage or a business partnership, the chief executive–board chair relationship brings together two people with distinct personalities, experiences, preferences, perspectives, operating styles, and decision-making modes. Furthermore, both are proven leaders, meaning each also has healthy doses of self-confidence, vision, energy, and innovative ideas. Put them together, and you're bound to have disagreements.

How those disagreements play out within the organization and are ultimately resolved will set the tone for the board chair's term in office. Allowing tensions to build and spill over into relationships with other board and staff members can create divided loyalties and unwelcome schisms. Everyone devotes his or her time to rehashing or second guessing what one of the leaders said or did instead of focusing on the business at hand.

Agreeing to disagree, and acknowledging that you are equal partners, is a big step forward on the journey called nonprofit management.

It Takes Two

Talk to any nonprofit board chair or chief executive involved in a true partnership of leadership, and you're bound to hear one message:

It takes mutual trust. The board chair must trust his or her own abilities to fulfill the job's many responsibilities and trust the chief executive to do the same, and vice versa.

Of course, arriving at that level of trust is easier said than done. Rarely does it simply happen on its own. If you recognize that a problem exists within the partnership, that's half the battle. Chances are your partner in leadership has come to a similar conclusion. Both of you can take steps to build or restore trust and keep the organization moving ahead.

Review your respective roles and responsibilities. Every board and staff member can probably recite the mantra: The board handles strategy, while the staff handle operations. But what does that mean?

Simply put, the board is responsible for the ends and the staff are responsible for the means. To use a nautical analogy, the board determines where the organization needs to head, charts the appropriate course, and checks progress along the way. The staff, with the chief executive as its captain, move the organization toward its destination, taking care to avoid rough waters.

Because it is responsible for governance — including setting policies and goals, keeping the organization true to its mission, and monitoring performance — the board does not become involved in day-to-day operations. As board chair, the last thing on your mind should be hiring or firing staff members (with the exception of the chief executive), doling out assignments to employees, or picking out the carpet for the organization's redecorated conference room.

Conversely, the chief executive concentrates on implementing board decisions, not publicly disagreeing with them or ignoring outright the decisions that he or she doesn't personally approve. As the board revises strategies and goals, the chief executive must go with the flow and restructure the staff or take on new tasks accordingly. For instance, a staff structured to support growth in fundraising will look different than one with an intense focus on program delivery.

Talking through difficult situations from the perspective of your differing roles can illuminate how best to approach a resolution. One nonprofit executive, for example, got wind of dissatisfaction among voting delegates regarding one of the names on the organization's slate of nominees for the board. With the annual meeting a few days away, she called the board chair to discuss alternatives. Both agreed a contested election would split the delegates into factions and could derail the organization's recent progress. Both also knew their roles. While the chief executive worked behind the scenes, preparing for any eventuality at the meeting itself, the board chair called a meeting of the executive committee and the board nominee and then followed up with calls to the most vocal delegates, speaking volunteer to volunteer. The election went off without a hitch.

Even if your partnership has already begun, consider attending a seminar or workshop specifically for elected leaders and staff executives. Both of you might gain valuable insights into the other's leadership or management style. Plus, simply spending time together can make you more comfortable conversing and working with one another. Knowing your boundaries, as prescribed by your respective job descriptions, will make you less likely to overstep them.

Review the organization's strategic plan. What are the strategic priorities for the year? If the board and staff have agreed on what the organization will do (annual operating objectives) and how much it will spend (annual operating budget), then both the chief executive and the board chair will have their work cut out for them. There won't be time (or money) for either to launch a new initiative merely on a whim.

Focusing on the strategic plan underscores the common ground on which both parties operate. As different as your personal approaches may be, you are working toward the same goal: the organization's success.

Spend time on the other person's turf. Some organizations have a tradition of inviting the newly elected board chair to spend a day at headquarters — not just sitting in the chief executive's office but meeting with employees and getting a feel for how the organization operates. In turn, the chief executive may spend a day in the board chair's environment, to gain a better understanding of the daily pressures he or she faces in addition to volunteer responsibilities.

The insights gained from watching the other person at work can help forge a stronger partnership. In fact, each person may come away from the trading places experience feeling thankful for his or her own responsibilities and with many ideas on how to better communicate and work with the other partner.

FOSTERING COMMUNICATION

Communicate with your partner about what you are doing on behalf of the organization, whom you have talked to about what, and what upcoming commitments are on your calendar (such as speaking engagements, meeting with nonprofit colleagues, or conducting orientation for board nominees).

Set up a communication schedule. After reviewing your individual roles, responsibilities, and commitments, discuss the best way to stay in touch. One nonprofit chief executive has a standing appointment with his board chair: They talk by phone every Wednesday morning at 10 a.m. His schedule with another board chair was completely different, calling for the two to exchange daily e-mails (even just to say that nothing needed to be discussed).

Be open and honest. Telling the full story, rather than protecting your partner with half-truths, can prevent a small problem from escalating into a full-blown crisis. A partner in possession of all the facts is better able to weigh the options available and choose the most appropriate one.

Serve as role models. Both board and staff members will take their cues from their respective leader. If the board chair and chief executive bad-mouth one another or circumvent the other's authority by taking problems directly to other board or staff members, the whole environment will be tense and antagonistic. But a collegial culture will take root in organizations where the board chair and chief executive work as a team and support and applaud one another's efforts and accomplishments.

Both parties serve as role models within the community as well. How they present themselves and speak about one another reflects on the organization and gets noticed by donors, dues-paying members, reporters, and the general public.

INJECTING OBJECTIVITY

If you truly feel you have reached an impasse with your leadership partner, talk over the situation with a third party. The board chair may consult another board member, and the chief executive may turn to another nonprofit executive for a fresh perspective. If the tensions and problems remain, consider calling in an organizational consultant or a mediator skilled in conflict resolution, someone both parties can agree upon.

That's the route one nonprofit took when it became painfully obvious that the chief executive and board chair simply didn't like one another. Their constant sniping and griping had come close to paralyzing the board and the staff; everyone knew about the mutual dislike but tiptoed around the problem. One board member suggested hiring a facilitator, who had no previous contact with the organization. The facilitator used his objectivity and skills to identify and bring issues out into the open, rather than sweeping them under the rug. Ultimately, the two leaders discussed the situation, shook hands, and acknowledged to the rest of the board that the organization's goals would take precedence over their personal differences.

Board Chairs: Food for Thought

Regardless of how much leadership experience or professional expertise you have, serving as the board chair is unlike any other job. Even veteran leaders, who have served as the chief elected officer of more than one organization, often comment on how different each position is because of the different mission, objectives, strategies, and personalities involved. Just remember you're not alone. The chief executive reports to the board, not just to you; the board, not you on your own, establishes policies, sets strategic direction, monitors organizational performance, and evaluates its own effectiveness.

Below are suggestions for making the most of your term.

Revisit the Organization

No matter how long you have been involved in the organization or served on its board, take the time to re-read key documents: bylaws, articles of incorporation, board policies, and the strategic plan. Also look over the previous year's financial statements, annual report, and audit. You've undoubtedly seen all of these before, but not necessarily through the eyes of the board chair. Brush up on parliamentary procedure as well so you feel comfortable running meetings.

Set Personal Goals

Every board chair wants to be remembered for accomplishments, not failures. But leaving your indelible mark on the organization should not come at the expense of its overall objectives. More than one organization has lost ground in a fundraising campaign or failed to develop a key initiative because the board chair had a pet project that siphoned off valuable financial and staff resources. And, more often than not, those projects become distant memories just a few years later.

To leave a lasting legacy, link your personal goals to the organization's overall agenda. Zero in on the one or two areas where you believe you can be most effective, then discuss what you'd like to accomplish with the chief executive. One board chair, for instance, made it his priority to streamline board operations so that decision makers felt more engaged. Working with the chief executive and the executive committee, he spearheaded bylaws changes that reduced the size of the board by 30 percent, cut the number of standing committees in half, and reduced the number of annual board meetings. Attendance at board and committee meetings rose, and recruitment of new board members no longer presented a problem.

State Your Preferences

As well as you may know each other, the chief executive isn't a mind reader. If you don't want to be bothered by ten e-mails or five phone calls from the chief executive every day, say so, and offer an alternative means of communication. If you'd rather not do a lot of public speaking or testify before elected officials, share that feeling so someone else can cover for you. If you think board meetings take too long, consult with the chief executive on how you can change the status quo.

When it comes to management of the organization, however, your preferred style or way of doing business doesn't matter. The day-to-day operations remain the chief executive's responsibility.

Assume the Best

When the chief executive responds to a suggestion by saying, "I'm not sure that's a good idea," don't jump to the conclusion that he or she is out to undermine your authority or push through a personal agenda. More likely, the chief executive has a good financial or operational reason and will explain it if given the chance. The advice is for you to take or leave, but the fact that it's offered is proof of a healthy partnership.

CHIEF EXECUTIVES: FOOD FOR THOUGHT

Nonprofit boards tend to place the responsibility for maintaining healthy board–staff relationships on the chief executive. After all, he or she is the constant in the equation: A board chair may come and go every year or two, while the chief staff executive may remain at the organization's helm for five, ten, or even twenty years.

Suggestions for building a strong partnership are discussed below.

Start Early

It's not unusual for a chief executive to begin working closely with the incoming board chair three to six months in advance. That provides the time to iron out any obvious problems and set up an effective communication system.

Even better, make an effort to acquaint yourself with the executive committee and other up-and-coming leaders in the organization. The next board chair will likely come from those ranks, so you can get a head start on developing a mutually beneficial partnership.

Avoid Power Struggles

The chief executive's job description includes serving as an ambassador on behalf of the organization and maintaining relationships with external audiences. He or she may also serve as the chief spokesperson, or the board may ask the board chair to assume that responsibility. Revisit all of your respective roles and responsibilities to clarify who handles what. There's little, if anything, for an organization to gain when its two most prominent representatives jockey for public recognition or engage in a tug-of-war contest on an issue.

Minimize Surprises

Board members need to hear bad news as soon as possible. So if revenue from an event or fundraising campaign is trickling in more slowly than expected, alert the board chair, seek his or her counsel, and mention your concern to the rest of the board (and discuss what staff are doing to address the problem). Don't wait until the quarterly financial reports are updated to call the problem to the board's attention.

Share good news, too, so no one is caught unaware by the public announcement of a large contribution, a community recognition, or in-depth media coverage of a program or event.

Look toward the Future

Monitor the process as the nominating committee identifies potential board leaders and develops a succession plan. Alert committee members to anyone who is so difficult to work with that you don't believe the resulting partnership would be as strong as the board and organization deserve.

Encourage Evaluation

If the board does not already have a formal process in place for evaluating chief executive performance, make that a priority in your discussions with the board chair. It's better to uncover any misunderstandings, unmet expectations, or performance issues during the evaluation process so they can be addressed, rather than be blindsided by a board's vote of no confidence.

Meet with the evaluation committee or task force — not just the board chair — to discuss the results and explain how you plan to improve any deficient areas. Also use the discussion to clarify performance targets for the coming year, especially how they relate to operational objectives and budget accountability.

CONFRONTATIONS CAN BECOME FRONT-PAGE NEWS

CASE IN POINT: AMERICAN RED CROSS

Washington, D.C.

Following the tragic events of September 11, 2001, people across the United States looked for ways to assuage their grief. Many chose to donate millions of dollars and countless pints of blood to the American Red Cross, placing their trust in a nonprofit organization with a long history of helping those affected by disasters.

As *The New York Times Magazine* noted, however, "At a moment when the Red Cross was supposed to be absorbed with ministering to a nation in crisis, it was confronting an internal crisis of its own making." Just six weeks after September 11, the chief executive of American Red Cross, Dr. Bernadine Healy, was without a job and the 120-year-old organization's reputation was taking a pounding in the media.

What happened? Small, unresolved conflicts built upon one another and gnawed away at any trust that may have existed between the chief executive and elected leaders. As roles and responsibilities blurred, a crisis was inevitable.

In the year before the American Red Cross hired Healy, its executive committee had taken a hands-on approach to managing operations. It was a task the committee appeared reluctant to give up after the interim chief executive had departed. David McLaughlin, the board chair, was quoted as acknowledging that the board was overstepping its role and authority. The board itself had 50 members — arguably an unwieldy number — with some drawn from corporations, government, and academia but the majority coming from the grass roots of local Red Cross chapters. To further complicate the governance structure, some board members were appointed and the rest elected.

After the director and bookkeeper at a local Red Cross chapter were indicted for embezzling $1 million, several board members questioned Healy's decision to hire outside auditors in the first place and to turn the matter over to the local prosecutor. Some directors later second guessed the firing of two long-time employees who failed to dispatch emergency disaster teams to the Pentagon crash site on September 11.

Several months into the job, Healy was confronted by inspectors from the Food and Drug Administration (FDA) who questioned procedures related to blood donations at several Red Cross chapters and cited health and safety violations systemwide. The board had disclosed the FDA violations at one local blood center but told Healy the situation was an isolated case.

The American Red Cross has a long-standing policy that it doesn't raise funds for specific disasters. Funds collected in the wake of a large-scale disaster, such as an earthquake or flood, benefit those directly affected as well as support general relief efforts undertaken by the organization. After contributions began pouring in after September 11, Healy created the Liberty Fund, reportedly without consulting the board. It would provide cash for victims' families, which the Red Cross hadn't done before, and fund-related initiatives, such as the creation of a strategic reserve of frozen blood.

The public gave generously — eventually contributing more than $600 million — operating on the assumption that the entire Liberty Fund would assist September 11 victims. For its part, the Red Cross did not refute that perception.

For years the American Red Cross had opposed the exclusion of Israel's disaster relief organization from the international federation of Red Cross and Red Crescent societies. Healy took a firm public position on the issue, and the board voted to strengthen its message by withholding its $4.5-million annual dues to the federation. Later, in a closed-door session that excluded Healy, the board reversed its decision and voted to pay the dues.

By then, thanks to internal correspondence leaked to the media, the public had become aware that their donations to the Liberty Fund were not necessarily going to victims of the September 11 tragedy. The Red Cross further fueled the public's animosity by not acknowledging how high emotions ran on the issue and by sticking to its policy of not designating funds for specific disasters. The organization failed to accurately read the public, who clearly thought the magnitude of the September 11 events called for a different policy.

The media took the organization to task, and Congress, which granted the American Red Cross its charter, promptly convened a hearing. To top it all off, Healy and McLaughlin publicly disagreed on why she was leaving the organization; she reported being forced out, and he denied it.

In the face of public outrage, the American Red Cross reversed itself yet again. The board voted to continue withholding dues from its international federation and announced that the entire Liberty Fund would be used to assist victims and families of the September 11 terrorist attacks. Such indecision, coupled with the well-publicized internal clash of board members and the chief executive, left the American Red Cross with another big job: regaining the public's trust and restoring donors' faith in its mission.

In June 2002, the organization adopted fundraising guidelines that omit any mention of a particular disaster in print advertisements. To avoid criticism, the group also announced that it will ask donors to confirm their understanding of how their contributions are to be used.

"Who Brought Bernadine Healy Down?" by Deborah Sontag, *The New York Times Magazine*, December 23, 2001, pages 32–40, 52–55.

Suggested Action Steps

1. Have the board chair and chief executive attend a partnership-building seminar or conference and discuss specific ways to work more effectively together.

2. Incorporate a discussion of the board–staff partnership into orientation for new board members; make a clear distinction between the board's responsibility (determining the ends or results) and the staff's responsibility (develop the means within board parameters).

3. Develop a formal process for annually evaluating the chief executive's performance; the process should include appointing an evaluation committee or task force with several board members.

16.
Internal
Controls

We just discovered that our chief executive has been funding personal expenses from the organization's operating budget. How should we deal with this problem? And how can we prevent it from recurring?

Any nonprofit, large or small, can be the target of fraud. What's more, the illegal activity isn't necessarily confined to the chief executive's office. Anyone with access to financial transactions, from order-processing clerks to accounting managers to chief financial officers, can capitalize on opportunities to move money from the organization's coffers into their own pockets.

The most egregious instances have been well publicized, such as the employees of Goodwill Industries in California, who, with their families, stole more than $15 million in 20 years by selling goods for personal profit and by doing "creative accounting" to channel funds to nonexistent companies. The chief administrative officer of the Ohio division of the American Cancer Society attempted to flee the country after embezzling nearly $7 million in charitable contributions over the years. Smaller-scale fraud — say, losses of $100,000 or even $10,000 — may not make the national newspapers but it can be financially and emotionally devastating to a nonprofit that counts every penny and values its reputation.

The temptation may be to handle the situation internally and quietly ask for repayment and the employee's resignation. After all, once the media gets wind of financial malfeasance, your organization is sure to be front-page news and the resulting coverage could affect financial and volunteer support. But you must report the crime to the proper authorities. Just put yourself in the position of hiring a new chief executive: Wouldn't you want to know if that person had a history of fraud or embezzlement? If you allow the chief executive to depart without a proper investigation, he or she may victimize another nonprofit in the future.

APPROPRIATE OVERSIGHT

Instituting internal controls is part of risk management (see Chapter 12). Having controls in place lessens or eliminates opportunities for fraudulent activity. To minimize the potential for employee theft, a non-profit board can put appropriate safeguards in place, such as those described below.

BOARD AS FINANCIAL MONITOR

Emphasize the board's role in monitoring financial matters. As part of new board member orientation, review the position's fiduciary responsibilities. Even if some duties are delegated to staff, the board remains accountable for the organization's financial health and must ensure that it

- keeps accurate and up-to-date financial records

- prepares accurate and timely financial statements

NOT ABOVE SUSPICION

"I can't believe it!" is what most people say when they learn an employee has been stealing equipment or supplies, forging checks, perpetrating credit card fraud, or otherwise embezzling from a nonprofit. After thinking a few moments, however, they usually recall something unusual about the person's actions.

Several behaviors may point to fraudulent activity. Be on the lookout for an employee who

- continually hires and fires other employees, especially those with access to financial records

- often mentions being behind on work and needing to stay late or come in on weekends to catch up

- prepares and follows an annual budget

- effectively manages assets

- complies with federal, state, and local regulations and applicable reporting requirements

This accountability goes beyond telling the chief executive to make sure it all gets done. As one nonprofit discovered, trusting the chief executive to make all the financial decisions is unwise: After 14 years of rubber-stamping the chief executive's recommendations regarding budgets and expenses, the board discovered the organization was nearly $1.5 million in debt. To make up the shortfall, the board had to drastically cut staff and slash programs it had spent years developing.

To help board members feel more comfortable, consider bringing in a consultant to review and explain various financial information. The briefing should cover the accounting method used (cash versus accrual), statement of financial position (assets and liabilities), statement of activities (actual receipts and expenditures, usually compared to the budgeted amounts), and cash flow statement (what resources are available at a certain time). Your organization may also develop a capital expenditure budget to cover long-term assets that can be depreciated.

- has difficulty producing financial reports on schedule or responding to requests for receipts or account statements

- insists on personally handling certain tasks because no one else could figure out my system

- always meets with the auditors alone; discourages others from talking with auditors

- appears to have financial problems, perhaps related to drug or alcohol abuse or gambling debts

- gets caught in little white lies

- doesn't take vacations

- acquires an expensive habit or makes an extravagant purchase that seems beyond his or her means and openly talks about it

Cultivate an environment that encourages people to ask questions if they don't understand a term that's used or an explanation that's provided. If, for instance, the board chair asks for more detail on a large variance between actual and budgeted revenues, other board members will follow the lead and ask for clarifications or explanations as well.

To make well-informed financial decisions, board members also need to remain abreast of trends within the community and the nonprofit sector as a whole. Helpful benchmarks may include membership or donor retention rates, cost to acquire a new donor or member, average program or product costs, and what percentage of each dollar raised goes to program delivery versus administrative costs.

DELEGATE FINANCIAL REVIEWS TO COMMITTEE

Delegate in-depth review of finances to high-level committees. Unless they have a financial background, board members' eyes are likely to glaze over when presented with page upon page of numbers. To keep the board focused on the organization's overall financial picture, have the finance committee review and approve monthly and quarterly reports, the annual budget, the annual audit, and financial policies before their presentation to the board. Other responsibilities may include recommending an auditing firm and ensuring the organization meets its regulatory requirements. The treasurer serves as the committee's liaison to the board of directors.

Some organizations have a separate investment committee that, in consultation with the finance committee, looks at short- and long-term opportunities for growth (see Chapter 5). It's crucial that the committees reach beyond the board of directors for their members, ideally tapping volunteers who are bankers, accountants, or money managers.

Regardless of their expertise, both committees should forward recommendations to the board for approval, so the final decision and responsibility ultimately rest with the elected leadership. Engage board members more fully by presenting the financial information visually, formatted as user-friendly charts and graphs to support recommendations. One nonprofit's treasurer even made a habit of including photographs and cartoons within her board presentations, just to keep board members alert to the numbers being reviewed.

INSTITUTE CHECKS AND BALANCES

While you don't want board members involved in day-to-day operations, such as signing all checks prepared by staff, implement policies to govern large transactions or decisions with financial implications. For instance, you might require the chief executive and board chair to co-sign checks over the amount of $10,000. Transferring funds from one account to another may require the approval of one or two executive committee members. A member of the executive or finance committee might have the responsibility of meeting with the chief executive and the auditor to review the firm's findings and specific recommendations, without other employees present. Ultimately, the full board should meet with the auditor and be able to ask questions directly. This practice enforces the sense of fiduciary duty that each board member needs to embrace.

Ensure that internal systems also include fraud controls. For example, the person who opens the envelopes containing charitable contributions should not be the same person who records the contributions or deposits them in the bank. Whoever signs the checks should not also balance the bank statement each month. Although such procedures may seem cumbersome, especially in a nonprofit with a small staff, they can reduce temptation for would-be embezzlers.

ESTABLISH HUMAN RESOURCES POLICIES

Check employment references and credentials. Employees who commit fraud rely on lies, so they are likely to submit a resume with fictitious employment or achievements. Trust your intuition if you are uncomfortable with someone's explanation of a gap in employment or educational credentials. A few phone calls might uncover a pattern of deception.

Make sure employees are bonded, as appropriate. Every employee who comes in contact with money, including part-time and temporary hires, should fall into this category.

Develop an employee code of conduct. Ask each employee to review and sign a document agreeing to ethical behavior. Although this won't stop anyone intent on committing a crime, it will make other employees aware of the importance your organization places on honesty and good moral conduct. In such a culture, employees are more likely to report something suspicious or outright deceitful.

CHECK WITH YOUR INSURANCE COMPANY

Find out whether your current policy offers crime protection for forgery, theft of money, and other crimes, and how much the policy would pay. Based on your insurance agent's recommendations, you might want to increase the coverage.

Your auditor may have additional fraud-prevention suggestions tailored to fit your organization's size, structure, and type of operations. As an objective outsider, the auditor can more clearly identify areas where employees, suppliers, or volunteers could easily engage in wrongdoing. Just don't rely solely on your auditor to detect fraud. Although auditors do spot-checks of selected statements and documents as part of the annual audit, they are not necessarily looking for fraudulent activity. Plus, they work from the documents and explanations provided by staff members who may have something to hide.

WHAT TO DO

If you and other board members suspect fraud within your organization, or if an employee has raised the subject with you, quietly gather evidence. Look for altered documents, conflicting financial statements, payments to companies the organization does not do business with, and so forth. Should the evidence point to a long-standing pattern of deceit, arrange for a forensic audit that looks back several years.

Guard against making any public statements that could be construed as slander. If your assumptions prove incorrect or if you need more time to gather evidence, your statements could put you at legal risk.

Assuming you have evidence of wrongdoing in hand, call local law enforcement officials to report the crime and stop the thief in his or her tracks. The chief executive should handle this if the fraud involves another employee; the board chair should make the call if the chief executive is suspected. If the crime violates federal laws, the Federal Bureau of Investigation may become involved as well.

Call your insurance company; depending on your policy, losses may not be covered unless you notify law enforcement officials. Also, activate your crisis management plan (see Chapter 14) to minimize damage to the organization's reputation.

Internally, employees and board members who were deceived by the thief can benefit from talking about the experience in individual or group counseling sessions; they often feel betrayed and unhappy about continuing in their positions. If criminal charges are filed, your organization may request restitution from the former employee. That may help ease others' minds and restore the public's trust.

On a Spending Spree

Case in Point: Catholic Charities of San Francisco

San Francisco, California

Between 1998 and 2000, Catholic Charities of San Francisco reimbursed its chief executive for more than $73,000 in expenses that were unrelated to his professional post. Specifically, the organization paid for lavish meals, laser hair-removal treatments, and BOTOX injections provided by a plastic surgeon to remove facial wrinkles. Because the chief executive's assistant approved his expense reimbursements, presumably assigning the costs to various internal accounts, the board did not immediately realize the extent nor the inappropriateness of the extravagance.

Eventually, the truth emerged. Confronted by the board, the chief executive resigned. Although he repaid the plastic surgery costs, the chief executive was not asked to reimburse the organization for any of the $51,000 spent on meals — some of which he had eaten alone, not with community leaders as noted on the expense reimbursements.

The cost for lax internal controls climbed higher, however. At least one funding agency reduced its payment to Catholic Charities by $1 million, with other donors rethinking their support as well. The next chief executive hired by Catholic Charities had a clear mandate: Restructure the organization to tighten financial controls and to provide more oversight by the board.

Suggested Action Steps

1. Appoint several board members to meet with the auditor, without staff present, to review internal controls and identify any areas in which controls are lacking.

2. Have a process in place through which employees can report suspected fraud without fear of reprisal.

17.

Boards and
the Big Picture

Our board meetings drag on and on because several members insist on focusing on minutiae, usually operational in nature. Rather than roll our eyes at each trivial question, what can the rest of us do?

It's not unusual for board members, especially those from the grassroots of an organization, to blur the line between governance and operations. They know they have been elected to help lead the organization, which requires a big-picture perspective. However, their expertise is in the field, with other operational volunteers, and perhaps their hearts remain there as well.

These dedicated volunteers probably know employees by name, especially in organizations with a small staff, and have more than a passing familiarity with programs and services that other board members know only by a line in a budget. In that regard, their insights are invaluable, provided they know when to take off the volunteer hat and put on the governance hat.

MICROMANAGEMENT: SYMPTOMS AND CURE

When do board members cross the line between governing the organization and managing operations? When their behavior, while functioning in the role of a board member, includes such things as

- offering unsolicited opinions on purchases of office equipment or selection of vendors

- becoming involved in personnel issues, such as hiring and firing staff (other than the chief executive) or approving salary increases

- demanding to review invoices and receipts

- creating a committee that deals with operational issues already assigned to staff

- sitting in, uninvited, on staff meetings

Clarifying the distinct roles of staff and board members during the board orientation may reduce the potential for micromanagement by volunteers. Note that just because they can do something doesn't mean they should.

Although it's certainly appropriate for a board to make the decision on where the organization's new office will be located, it's not appropriate for the board to select the office decor or design the sign for the front door. Likewise, the board's responsibilities include approving budgets for specific programs; they do not include proofreading the marketing materials or deciding what will be served for lunch. Emphasize that engaging in the board's true work of governance, which usually includes serving on a committee or two, leaves no time for participating in staff decisions. Staff should understand the role of board members as well, so they don't unwittingly ask questions or provide information that pull governance volunteers into management functions.

Review the agendas for board meetings to ensure you're not unwittingly promoting micromanagement. Are the topics related to strategic goals rather than administrative issues? Do supporting materials present high-level information and thus facilitate big-picture discussion? When management issues appear on the agenda, for discussion or approval, board members will take that as an invitation to comment upon operational matters.

Another option is to find a means to involve the micromanaging board member in the area of his or her greatest interest. Suppose a board member often asks detailed questions about the organization's hardware, software, and computing capabilities. Consider appointing that person to serve on an operational task force that would develop overall policies and procedures for upgrading and maintaining the information technology system, or invite him or her to be the expert advisor to staff. Or give the person a challenge outside his or her comfort zone, such as helping develop a long-range plan, to channel energy and attention away from operations and toward strategic direction. Such focused participation might help the person feel more engaged in the board's overall work.

FOSTERING A STRATEGIC PERSPECTIVE

The best way to keep micromanagement by the board in check is to prevent it from ever taking hold. A chief executive can help focus the board on governance by working with the board chair to

- **Periodically review progress on the strategic plan.** Emphasize how the chief executive, in conjunction with staff, carries out the board's decisions. The report should focus on where the organization is headed, as determined by the board, and how that goal will be achieved, as determined by the chief executive.

- **Schedule a board retreat every two or three years.** Revisit the organization's mission and vision. At the retreat, the board members should deal with long-term questions such as: What developing trends will shape the organization in the next five to ten years? Where do we as an organization want to be in five years? Whom do we want to be serving? How will we know if we have succeeded? What can we do now to increase our chances of success in the future?

- **Structure meeting agendas to minimize operational reports.** Offer to supply comprehensive supporting documents later should board members request more details. Group housekeeping items, such as approval of previous minutes and committee appointments, in a consent agenda. This frees up time for higher-level discussion. In fact, some chief executives include two or three strategic questions under each agenda item to get board members thinking in advance about what comments or feedback to offer.

- **Aim for a give-and-take dialogue between staff and the board at meetings.** Instead of having staff answer a string of detailed questions fired off by board members, the chief executive can facilitate discussion and summarize the strategic points made by board members, perhaps by politely asking, "Where are we right now in the discussion? How do these comments relate to the strategic issue at hand?"

- **Develop visual indicators of organizational performance.** Charts and graphs can help the board easily gauge progress. For instance, the board may receive frequent updates on the progress of a capital campaign or a membership drive, with comparison data from previous years or comparable organizations.

- **Integrate a board development activity into every meeting.** This may range from a presentation by an outside financial expert or staff program specialist to an overview of funding within your community to a personal story shared by a client or member served by the organization. Another option is to break the board into smaller groups for roundtable discussions on topics related to mission and vision, then reconvene to process the information that emerged from the brainstorming.

- **Evaluate the board's own performance.** Some groups do a quick check-in after every meeting or two, asking board members to rate, on a continuum, the level of discussion (operational versus strategic), the issues covered (trivial versus significant), and the materials provided (useless versus useful). Others periodically ask community members, staff, and clients or customers to provide feedback on how well the organization appears to be governed.

- **Conduct exit interviews.** When board members complete their terms or resign, exit interviews can help you identify areas in which board orientation and meetings themselves might be improved. Questions may include the following:

  - How much did the board focus its energies on fulfilling the organization's mission?

  - How well were your expertise and abilities used during your term in office?

  - How do you feel you have contributed to the board's work? To the organization as a whole?

  - Did you have any disappointments in relation to your role as a board member?

  - Do you believe the expectations outlined before you became a board member matched the reality of the position?

  - Do you believe you received all the training you needed to serve effectively on the board? If not, what would have benefited you the most?

  - What subject areas or committees interest you the most? How might the organization continue to draw on your skills?

Although the board chair has the task of keeping the discussion focused on strategic issues, he or she may welcome support if an individual insists on micromanaging. Encourage other board members to speak up if they believe a meeting is getting off track or the board is delving unnecessarily into operational details.

Ideally, the chief executive and the board chair tackle micromanagement issues together. In fact, their partnership should mirror their message that the board governs and the staff implements. After talking through their concerns about a micromanaging board member, the leaders should jointly generate a solution. The board chair may need to talk with the member, volunteer to volunteer, while the chief executive may adjust how much information is presented or the way it is communicated.

Of course, the board chair may be the micromanager. In that case, the chief executive needs to initiate a one-on-one discussion about appropriate roles and responsibilities. If other board members also believe the board chair is getting bogged down in details, consider calling in a facilitator to lead a board self-evaluation and get everyone thinking about ways to improve.

Should the entire board favor micromanagement, that can be a sure sign that no one has confidence in the chief executive's ability to manage the organization. A hands-on approach by the board may be warranted in a crisis or transition situation, such as when the chief executive has resigned or been fired for financial mismanagement. However, this tactic must end when a replacement is hired. Then it's up to the new chief executive to partner with the board chair, communicate effectively with the entire board, and manage staff and operations smoothly. That can keep meddling to a minimum.

Suggested Action Steps

1. When developing agendas and advance materials for board meetings, make sure they do not emphasize operational issues nor open the door to discussions of minutiae.

2. Keep board members focused on their governance responsibilities by incorporating board development or educational activities into meetings, such as presentations by guest experts or constituents.

Resources

Andringa, Robert C., and Ted W. Engstrom. *Nonprofit Board Answer Book* (expanded edition). Washington, D.C.: BoardSource, 2001.

Angelica, Emil. *Crafting Effective Mission & Vision Statements*. St. Paul, Minn.: Amherst H. Wilder Foundation, 2001.

BoardSource. *Unlocking Profit Potential*. Washington, D.C.: BoardSource, 2002.

Coffey, John, Valerie Garrow, and Linda Holbeche. *Reaping the Benefits of Mergers and Acquisitions*. Boston: Butterworth-Heinemann, 2002.

Cox, John B., Editor. *Professional Practices in Association Management*. Washington, D.C.: American Society of Association Executives, 1997.

Dees, J. Gregory, Jed Emerson, and Peter Economy. *Enterprising Nonprofits: A Toolkit for Social Entrepreneurs*. New York: John Wiley & Sons, 2001.

Dees, J. Gregory, Jed Emerson, and Peter Economy. *Strategic Tools for Social Entrepreneurs*. New York: John Wiley & Sons, 2002.

Dietel, William M., and Linda R. Dietel. *The Board Chair Handbook*. Washington, D.C.: BoardSource, 2001.

Eadie, Douglas C. *The Board-Savvy CEO*. Washington, D.C.: BoardSource, 2001.

Eadie, Douglas C. *The Extraordinary CEO*. Washington, D.C.: American Society of Association Executives, 1999.

Friedman, Thomas L. *The Lexus and the Olive Tree*. New York: Farrar, Straus and Giroux, 1999.

Herman, Melanie L., and Leslie T. White. *Leaving Nothing to Chance: Achieving Board Accountability through Risk Management*. Washington, D.C.: BoardSource, 1998.

Hopkins, Bruce R. *The Legal Answer Book for Nonprofit Organizations*. New York: John Wiley & Sons, 1996.

Hopkins, Bruce R. *Starting & Managing a Nonprofit Organization*. New York: John Wiley & Sons, 2001.

Kurtz, Daniel L. *Managing Conflicts of Interest.* Washington, D.C.: BoardSource, 2001.

Larson, Rolfe. *Venture Forth! The Essential Guide to Starting a Moneymaking Business in Your Nonprofit Organization.* St. Paul, Minn.: Amherst H. Wilder Foundation, 2002.

National Association of Corporate Directors. *Information Security Oversight: Essential Board Practices.* Washington, D.C.: National Association of Corporate Directors, 2001.

Olson, Robert, and Atul Dighe. *Exploring the Future: Seven Strategic Conversations That Could Transform Your Association.* Washington, D.C.: American Society of Association Executives, 2001.

Simmons, Karen, and Gary J. Stern. *Creating Strong Board-Staff Partnerships.* Washington, D.C.: BoardSource, 1999.

Sorrells, Michael, and Andrew S. Lang. *The IRS Form 990: A Window into Nonprofits.* Washington, D.C.: BoardSource, 2001.

Szanton, Peter. *Evaluation and the Nonprofit Board.* Washington, D.C.: BoardSource, 1998.

Train, John, and Thomas A. Melfe. *Investing and Managing Trusts under the New Prudent Investor Rule.* Boston: Harvard Business School Press, 1999.

Vowell, Susan S. *The Complete Guide to Managing Chapter Funds.* Washington, D.C.: American Society of Association Executives, 2000.

ABOUT THE AUTHOR

Robert C. Andringa Ph.D., has trained thousands of board members and their chief executives as president of The Andringa Group. His distinguished career includes service as a congressional committee staff director, CEO of the Education Commission of the States, policy director for a governor, founder of CEO Dialogues, Inc., and service on numerous national boards and advisory groups. Currently, he serves as president of the Council for Christian Colleges & Universities, an association of 150 institutions in 17 countries.